James Lawson

Liddesdale

The Border Chief

James Lawson

Liddesdale
The Border Chief

ISBN/EAN: 9783337340780

Printed in Europe, USA, Canada, Australia, Japan

Cover: Foto ©Thomas Meinert / pixelio.de

More available books at **www.hansebooks.com**

LIDDESDALE

OR

THE BORDER CHIEF

A TRAGEDY

DRAMATIS PERSONÆ.

LORD LIDDESDALE.

JOHNSTONE, OF LOCHWOOD,	*A Friend to Liddesdale.*
LORD HUME, ...	*In Love with Lady Christina.*
KER, OF CESSFORD, . .	*A Friend of Lord Hume.*
LORD MAXWELL, . . .	*An Old Lord.*
MASTER OF MAXWELL, .	*His Son, beloved by Lady Christina.*
SIR JOHN CHARTERS, .	*The Scottish Warden.*
WILLIAM LORD DACRE, . .	*The English Warden.*
CARNEGIE, ...	*A Vassal of Maxwell, feigning a Mute.*
KENNETH, ...	*An Old Domestic.*
A PRIEST, ...	*Confessor to Lady Christina.*

A HERALD.

LADY CHRISTINA,	*Daughter of Liddesdale.*
MABEL,	*Her Nurse.*

Heralds, Mosstroopers, Peasants, Lords, Soldiers, etc.

Scene in Liddesdale.
Part *of the Third Act in Carlisle.*

LIDDESDALE.

ACT I.

Scene I.—Liddel Castle.

Enter Kenneth *and* Mabel.

Ken. Peace, peace, good Mabel.

Mab. That ever I was born to see this day !

Ken. I am an old man, and in my three-score years I
never found any good come of believing in dreams.

Mab. A little child, trembling at the winter's hearth, I
believed in them. They say in sleep the immortal
soul may read as in parables, revealment of the
future.

Ken. You make me almost believe in **your** fear; tho'
it is a foolish fear.

Mab. And then the legend !

> When cruel might
> Down-crushes right:
> When humble foes
> And high oppose—
> Listen the wail
> Of Liddesdale !

Ken. A silly rhyme. But what was the dream?

Mab. I thought I was awake—it seemed so like noon-day truth— I was I know not when nor where : all things gloomed darkly : I saw them dimly, as through the storm-cloud we mark the sun in the sky. Suddenly I stood in the White chamber : it was brightly lighted with beaming eyes; glad voices spoke, and merry music sounded—but in a moment, darkness—thick, deep darkness—shrouded all.

Ken. Why, this is not so terrible, Mabel. I read good bodement here. This foreshows the marriage of our dear young lady with the Master of Maxwell. We shall all be so happy that day, Mabel.

Mab. But hear me Kenneth ; I ran to the window to let daylight in—the sky was overcast, not with dark dun clouds that threaten rain or storm, but blood-red clouds, weeping thick crimson drops.

Ken. A dreaming fancy of the wounded deer, that fell yesterday at your feet and died.

Mab. No, Kenneth ; woe is me, no ! Then I saw a proud eagle pounced on by a wicked hawk; its beak and talons tore it deep, deep and deeper, till blood—the very color of the clouds—oozed out.

Ken. This is the falcon-hunt fretting thy resting hours —many strong-winged birds, that day, were like the eagle of your dream.

Mab. At last the hawk tore out the eagle's heart, and shook it revengefully at a cooing dove perched on a blighted rowan-tree. The innocent moaned a bitter moan, and fell down—dead upon the ground.

Ken. What of the hawk, then?

Mab. I saw no more; tears blinded my eyes: Oh! woe is me, I saw no more; but a voice in the air murmured the legend—bitterly, Kenneth, bitterly.

Ken. Art well this morning? Last night thou wert feverish and disturbed in sleep. Where is the quaigh? Good Mabel, let me fill it with usquebaugh—thou wilt not, that by thy pillow, have such dreams again.

Mab. You are kind, and usquebaugh is very wholesome. You do not reverence dreams, Kenneth?

Ken. I cannot say that I do, Mabel; but I hold it no less than heresy to doubt Witches, Ghosts and Spirits; our Lord and Lady, their forebears too, believed in them. These we may not doubt.

Mab. No, truly. But the usquebaugh?

Ken. When comes the Master of Maxwell?

Mab. My lady looks for him at noon. I hope our Chief will be kind; but why he brings Lord Hume so often to the castle I know not. What do you think?

Ken. We must not question our Chief's intents—we must obey his will. But Lord Hume looks on our dear young mistress with an eye of favor.

Mab. Ah, Kenneth! never will she give her love for his; he is not gentle like the brave young Maxwell. He has not such an eye; no, nor such a smile.

Ken. Well, well! Bless her innocent soul! Vex her
    no more with thy idle dreamings, Mabel.

Mab. You spoke of usquebaugh!

Ken. You shall have the quaigh, full—and a Brancher
    pie besides.

Mab. It is their season—nearly. Usquebaugh is very
    wholesome.   [*Exeunt.*

SCENE II.—*A woody, wild and mountain pass.   Bugles.
    A March.   Enter* LORD HUME, KER, *of Cessford,*
    JOHNSTONE, *of Lochwood and followers.*

Loch. Well, here we are before him.   Patience, friends;
    If he come not at the appointed moment,
    An honest cause I warrant hath detained him.

Cess. The Three Estates are suddenly convened,
    And Liddesdale, perchance, delays to learn
    If pliant tools have passed the threatened law.

Loch. Dare they?   For what?   To please a baby king,
    A froward boy, who under age is crowned.

Hume. With justice fired, our sovereign seems resolved
    To turn reformer and amend the world.

Cess. The English mother's, and French uncle's sway,
    During a long minority, he swears
    Has soured the nobles, nurtured discontent,
    And spread disloyalty throughout the realm.

Hume. Cursed is the country with an infant king.

Cess. That in especial on the borders, here,

In derogation of the sovereign power,
We have usurped the law and dared chastise
The English thieves and beat them to their homes.

Loch. What else, sir, should we do? Look tamely on,
With visor up and sword undrawn, and thank
The greedy knaves for ravaging our lands?
Or, in the spirit of our fathers, rise
And strike the invaders down?

Cess. No, Lochwood, no:
But we at Holy-rood should humbly kneel,
Weep o'er our wrongs, and pray the honored king
Would graciously vouchsafe his royal aid,
And shield us from injustice!

Loch. Very true!
I did not think of that: but I am blunt;
Some say, discourteous. May the wrath of heaven
Strike me this instant dead, ere I would court
The aid of man, though twenty times a king.
What says Lord Hume?

Hume. I pray you, pardon me:
My mind was wandering.

Loch. Cessford, thy ear:
Our friend, whose life is a romance—that is,
His thought turns woman-ward—is musing now
On fair Christina; she is worth the winning.

Hume. She is a maid as innocent and kind
As ever brushed the dew-drop from the flower,
Or graced the dance, the banquet or the chase.

1*

[A March.   Enter LIDDESDALE, CAR-
NEGIE, *Lords and followers.*

Liddes. Good morrow : 'save ye gentlemen and friends:
The sun rules fiercely in meridian height;
'Tis my appointed time.   Your grace awhile.
[*To Carnegie*] Thou knowest the pledge on which I
spared thy life,
Look to it well: if thou by breath or sign
Declare thou art not what thou feign'st—thou diest.
But faithful as my shadow thou must be,
The secret listener of my vassals' words,
That I, of all, may sure advantage take,
None dreaming of the source.   I cry your mercy.

Loch. Here have we waited noble Chief, to learn
The latest news of these disjointed times.

Liddes. 'Tis statute and ordained I am a traitor—
I, who ne'er stooped to a dishonest deed,
Nor ever left an injury unavenged !
Besides, in most opprobrious terms, my friends
Are held as contumacious to the king.

Cess. No, not to him, but to his evil counsellors
And laws unjust, stand we in opposition.

Loch. What treason talk they of ?

Liddes. It is alleged
That we in violation of the peace   [subjects;
With England's king, have robbed and slain his
That thereby old resentments are revived
Against the general safety of the realms.

Revived ! This hatred which the Borderers nurse,
Has been through time the motion of each heart,
And we shall cherish it, while Southron churls,
Stuffed to the throat, look on us with disdain.

Loch. I hate the English as I hate the devil.

Liddes. Our lands are now declared the common prey,
Our kinsmen thieves, and we, believe it, rebels,
To be pursued by sleuth-hound, fire and sword.
What ! are we aliens or intruders here,
That they dare hunt us like the ravenous wolves,
Or think to do it !

Loch. Are we crushed already !

Cess. Let them approach one step, and they shall learn
What men may do when conscious of the right.

Liddes. Yes, right!   When English knaves have
crossed the March,
And from our plenty stolen to fat their greed,
I slew them on the spot—if they escaped,
Pursued, and ten times retribution took.
For every Scotsman by a Southron slain,
I have made twenty bleed. This sacred right,
By all confessed, the right of self-defence,
Is termed a treason—and, start not to hear it,
At Edinburgh Cross they've put me to the Horn,
With phrase freebooter, added to my name.
Now, by my sword I swear, from this hour forth,
Here I renounce allegiance to the king ;
And not alone in my defence I stand,

But in his opposition. Judge me, friends,
And for yourselves resolve.

Cess. I am resolved.

Loch. And I. Rather than live his passive slave,
I would turn spae-wife and beg daily alms.

Liddes. Has not my noble Hume a word to say?
I met a friendly greeting from his eye,   [father
But nothing from his lips. What, dumb! Thy
Who suffered for the jealousies of state,
As thine did, Cessford—on the scaffold suffered—
He always had a word to spare a friend,
And if his need required, an arm to help.

Hume. My lord, excuse me : I was lost in thought.

Loch. The youth is wisely sparing of his speech ;
Secure his power: thy daughter is the price.

Liddes. I understand. Brave sir, we all have thoughts,
Sometimes unwelcome thoughts, that take the mind
A prisoner as it were, and shut it up
From the gay troop of pleasant memories
That sweeten life, and make us slow to pay
The courtesy we owe. Hast heard the news?

Hume. I have, with feelings of regret and pain;
For I suspect the true cause is concealed,
And a false motive meanly urged.

Liddes. What think'st?

Hume. Thou art too powerful: monarchs ever fear
A powerful subject.

Liddes. That is shrewdly said.

Hume. Why in especial art thou singled out
  For royal hate ? Thy independent mind
  By valiant clansmen aided, dares the right.
Liddes. And will maintain it, spite of priest or king.
Hume. Hence art thou feared, for this must be subdued;
  The sooner, surer, as the adage runs.
Cess. I marvel much this struck me not before ;
  The thought seems like an old familiar tune
  Forgotten long—but instantly when heard,
  Is recognized and loved.
Hume. The cause is plain—
  When French and English regents ruled the land,
  And fierce contention shook it to the centre,
  Thou stood'st aloof from profitless revolts,
  And used thy power to vindicate thy rank :
  While in the Lothians and the land of Fife,
  In the far Mearns and distant northern isles,
  Revenge and hate crushed Scotland's bravest men.
  And there, a weak nobility abide,
  Who for self-interest, or in fear, are loyal.
Liddes. Much wiser than thy years !
Loch. Old as I am,
  I never dreamed of this ! 'Tis gospel truth.
Cess. Words with electric fire, that rouse men up
  To deeds the world may look on and admire.
Hume. Like an old play revived, the present age
  Simply reacts the story of the past   [ment.
  With change of scene, but not perhaps, improve-

Wert thou subdued, he turns his arms 'gainst me,
In which succeeding, then comes Cessford's turn,
Or honest Lochwood, thine—singly we fall,
And our dear Scotland is a mart of slaves.

Loch. We must brush up our armor—that I see.

Cess. Which is the worst—endurance or redress?

Loch. Endurance : may annihilation come
Rather than base submission to our wrongs.

Liddes. Let him or his with hostile front approach,
Yea, let him step one inch upon my land,
And by my father's unattainted name,
He'll sorely rue the day,

Hume. If we succeed
The king is an oppressor, patriots we.
Success is sovereign law.

Liddes. Brave, noble youth !
Long have I looked with pride upon thy growth;
I see a spirit swelling in thy blood,
A courage in thy heart presaging greatness.

Hume. Sir, I will die to merit good men's praise.

Liddes. Not die, but fight thou may'st. I have a
treasure,
And dear to me as liberty or life—
A noble, brave and generous lord is he
Who wins her hand. Increase in thy desert,
And I may whisper in her gentle ear,
Thou art her father's friend.

Hume. Forever thine !

Cess. Hast heard the Wardens met last night in council?

Liddes. I hear it from my spies. With them convened
　　Time-serving nobles and faint-hearted chiefs:
　　A herald, as I learn, will soon proclaim
　　The foul decision of this Warden-Court.

Hume. Maxwell is in their confidence, 'tis said.

Liddes. The name of Maxwell is my seated hate,
　　And festers in my soul. One of his house
　　Once marched disdainful past my castle gate,
　　With pennon streaming and with visor closed,
　　With bugles sounding and with glaive unsheathed,
　　Despite all rule and token of respect.
　　This insult, in fit time, I shall avenge.

Hume. The Master is a visitor of thine.

Liddes. Doubt not, nor fear. I have already said
　　That I will whisper in my daughter's ear
　　Thy name and my regard.

Hume. My all, save honor,
　　Most gladly will I peril for her hand.

Liddes. I promise thee: no thanks. On to our Castle.
　　　　　　　　　　　　　　　　[*Exeunt.*

SCENE III.—LIDDEL CASTLE : *around the room and
　　on the wall are seen implements and trophies of
　　war and chase.* LADY CHRISTINA *engaged in
　　embroidery.*

Lady C. An idle dream! and yet the legend runs,
　　A sign will tell the downfall of our house.

On ride or raid my father is abroad ;
He is the last in whom exists our name,
No son has he to inherit his renown ;
And I a maid, when married, like a brook
Whose current mingles with some noble river,
Am then my former self no more.　Ah me !
Much I lament these wild, distracted times ;
For England's Henry, and old Scotland's James,
With frowning brows regard the border lords—
And then the history of my foolish heart,
Is chequered, like love's tale, with hopes and fears.

　　　　　　　　[*Enter* MABEL.

Come hither, nurse: sing me the " Bonny Page."
Mab. I cannot sing, and least of all that song.
Lady C. It is indeed a melancholy air :
　　The notes accord so sweetly with the verse,
　　They seem as one, both at a thought inspired—
　　And by the minstrel's magic power, they reach
　　The fount of feeling and subdue the heart.
Mab. Nay lady, do not sigh ; tell me what think'st ?
　　Does not young Maxwell love thee for thyself ?
　　Ah, now thou smilest !
Lady C. Thou art old and foolish.
Mab. There is a something in his beaming eye,
　　I know not what, that cheers and wins us all—
　　And when he speaks, no wonder woman loves.
　　May heaven bless him !
Lady C. An old enthusiast thou.

Behold the children on yon grassy knoll,
Health in their cheeks and pleasure in their eyes,
And every look is redolent of joy.
How lithe each limb! how earnest every bound!
No bitter thought through all the sunny hours,
No feverish dream through all the solemn night,
They touch the pillow and are blessed with sleep!
Hark to their gladsome voices!

Mab. I little thought,
When you, like them, ran on the velvet sward,
That I should live to see thy mind perplexed;
Nor did thy sainted mother, rest her soul! [*Hume,*

Lady C. Hush, Mabel, hush: my father comes, and
Whose presence is a pain: yet I must smile,
And mask with mirth the moaning of my heart.

    [*Enter* LIDDESDALE, HUME, LOCHWOOD
      and CESSFORD.

Liddes. My honored friends! We take her by surprise;
Her nurse and needle, signs of love and thrift,
You see beside her. Daughter, be thou kind. [*Aside.*]

Hume. How fares your ladyship?

Lady C. Unruly times
Scare timid women: save for these, I'm well.
From the chase my lord?

Hume. Yes, and fleet of foot
Were dogs and deer, that made the richer sport.

Liddes. More than the trophies of the chase, my child,
I bring for thee.

Lady C. Indeed!

Liddes. My heart's dear pride!

Lady C. What hast for me? for thou art ever kind.
I pray thee tell, nor overtask my guess.

Liddes. She *is* my daughter! Go, bid Kenneth bring—
He understands—I gave him charge withal.

                           [Exit MABEL.

Lady C. Thou would'st surprise me. Well! know'st
    thou, my lord?

Hume. I may not tell.

Lady C. Or thou?

Lochwood. I must be mute.

Lady C. What! mystery here! I shall be patient,
Incurious too—though it may shame the adage.

Liddes. Thou shalt be satisfied: they come.

      [Re-enter MABEL, *with* KENNETH *and* CARNEGIE.
           The Mute, at the motion of LIDDESDALE,
           kneels at the feet of LADY CHRISTINA.

Liddes. Thy page!
Daughter, I spared his life for thee.

Lady C. For me!

Liddes. An humble serf of not ungraceful mien:
I found him lurking in a secret pass,
And might have slain him had not chance revealed
He is a mute; for that I spared his life,
On one condition—'twas by signs expressed—
That he should serve thy bidding.

Lady C. Is he mute!

"*I must be mute*"—my lord, I understand.

Surely a novel present to a maid.

Liddes. A fancy, sweet, which thou may'st easier question

Than I make answer.

Lady C. Rise: I will be kind.

No tongue to speak, no ear to hear, alas!

Thou hast an eye; perchance a faithful heart,

Nobler, since utterance is denied.　Arise.

> [CARNEGIE *rises.*

Loch. It were a want important to a dame.

Lady C. My lord, take care, else I with worthy cause,

May challenge thy respect and love for us.

Loch. I am too old and tough to fret my mind

About the fairest maid in Christendom.

> [*Trumpets without.*

Liddes. I did not look for uninvited guests.

Who comes?

Mab. My lord;

> [LADY CHRISTINA *motions her to silence.*

Nay, I will speak the truth [*aside to her*].

Master of Maxwell we expect to-day.

Hume. Expected!

Liddes. Kenneth, bid him to our presence.　[*Exit* KEN.]

[*To Hume.*] To her we owe the first intelligence

Of his approach.

Lady C. [*Aside.*] Mabel, Mabel!

Cess. [*To Hume.*] What, jealous!

[*Re-enter* KENNETH *and* MASTER OF MAXWELL.

Liddes. Good morrow, sir.

Go give his retinue fit entertainment. [*Ex.* KENNETH.

M. of Max. Thanks for thy welcome: Good morrow,
[gentlemen.

How thrives the flower of Liddesdale to-day?

Lady C. I thank thee, well. Thy ride I hope was

M. of Max. With thoughts of thee.   [pleasant.

Hume. Observe, as she smiles on him,

The lustre of her eyes.

Loch. Yea, like love's torches

Of which the poet dreams—I never saw them.

Liddes. Be not, fair hostess, partial in your smiles;

If to each guest you mete not equal favor,

The welcome lacks both courtesy and grace.

Lady C. I thank you, father, for this admonition;

But latest come may claim the latest word:

That paid, to all I owe a like respect.

M. of Max. Carnegie! [*Aside.*]

Carn. Hush! [*Aside.*]

Liddes. Our hostess answers wisely.

Lady C. I cannot talk of chase or war in phrase

To match your cunning—but I have a fawn,

A falcon strong of wing, with jesses bound;

A hound well-shaped, whose speed is like the wind:

And in a cabinet of antique work

There are strange relics of the olden age,

Which speak a history of forgotten days.

Come with me, lords, come to the Eastern chamber;
And with impartial smiles, I will essay
To give a welcome worthy of my guests.

Liddes. Brave, dearly prized!

Loch. Or would ye imitate
The pious Abbot's sacrificing life,
Why cards, or dice, or tables ye may play,
And she, perchance, will join: in faith, I cannot.

M. of Max. Or chess, a game her gentleness admires.

Mab. And she, my lords, can play and sweetly sing,
And show such needlework.

Liddes. Her privilege!
Fond, babbling nurse, she thinks my daughter's skill
Should, in your sager judgment, as in her's,
Out-challenge all the world.

Mab. Mark well the tapestry that adorns the walls,
'Tis, I am told, the ancient Trojan tale;
Her dear hand wrought it all.

Liddes. Garrulous fool!
She deems the fancies that her lady's thought
Delights to linger with, should charm your minds;
As well might she enjoy our sterner moods—
But on, my noble friends.

[HUME *takes* LADY CHRISTINA's *hand.*

Lady C. Lead on, my lords.

[*Exeunt all except* CARNEGIE.

Carn. There is a guiding star to just revenge!

Man never yet was wronged, if he that's wronged,
Waited and watched, but found the avenging hour;
And this base lord shall feel my father's shame
In very kind.   And yet, my heart relents ;
Why should the guiltless for the guilty suffer !
If Maxwell speak, all's lost.   He is in danger :
Mine be the task to save him.   Grant, kind heaven,
That I may be an instrument of good,
Upholding justice and confounding crime ;
Grant my soul's wish, that this foul, lustful lord——
       [*Re-enter* LIDDESDALE.

Liddes. Why loiter here, why went not with the rest?
Carn. I waited thy command.
Liddes. Come hither sirrah !

   I doubt : nearer ! If false, make peace with heaven.
Carn. Preserver of my life—I am thy slave.
Liddes. Speak low, and feign as if by signs you spoke :
   I will not even trust my castle walls.

       [CARNEGIE *by signs professes devotion.*
   I will believe : if once I doubt, beware—
Sirrah, begone.

          [*Exit* CARNEGIE.
Freebooter I am called !
That sole addition to a name like mine
Stirs up my blood against the allied kings,
And never shall I slumber till avenged.
Lord Hume I must secure ; arrange her dower;
Which done, the clerk shall instantly engross.

Despite the legend, let what may befall,
I'll live the terror of each hostile chief,
And in the Borders rule, despite the king.

[*Exit.*

ACT II.

Scene I.—Liddel Castle.

Enter Lady Christina *and* Master of Maxwell.
Mabel, Kenneth *and* Carnegie *attending.*

M. of Max. Why dearest, art thou sad?   Tell me
                                      [the cause.
    I must assuage or else partake thy grief.
Lady C. Lately my father has expressed a wish
    That I should favor Hume.   I loath the man !
    His frequent visits courtesy endures,
    While all my thoughts turn to an absent one.
M. of Max. Turn they to me ?
Lady C. Why ask?   Thou know'st dear lord,
    Where all my fondest fancies stray.
M. of Max. I do,
    And in thy love the happiest of men.
Lady C. Lord Hume is powerful : in these stormy times
    My father needs his aid, and praises him,
    Not dreaming of our loves.
M. of Max. I am to blame ;
    I should ere this our secret have confessed
    And sought approval : but young blood is rash,
    And stops not to consult the frigid rules

Civility applauds. I will amend,
Seek him this moment and implore his blessing.

Lady C. I tremble : tell him (if in pliant mood,)
That I will never love another man.   [peace

M. of Max. Tho' stern of will, he would not risk thy
For twenty times twice told, the power of Hume.
Sweet one retire ; I hope ere daylight fades,
With his consent to claim thee for my bride.

Lady C. Go, speak with gentle and entreating words;
(For he is sometimes choleric when chafed,)
Perhaps thy asking may provoke his ire,
And he may rather chide than answer kindly :
If thou perceive the dawning of his anger,
Press not the subject, touch some other theme,
Grateful to his predominating mood.
Dear lord, adieu; I shall in patience wait
With anxious heart.

M. of Max. Give not a thought to fear,
For soon shall I a conqueror return
And take thee captive, thus. Till then, farewell.
     [*Exeunt* LADY CHRISTINA, MABEL *and* KENNETH.
Now sirrah, speak : thy presence is a marvel.

Carn. I will confess : Master, in whispers speak,
Listeners are round. I am thy father's vassal,
And thee, his first born, I would die to serve.

M. of Max. If that you tell shall be approved and true,
At any risk I will protect thy life.

Carn. Thou may'st perchance remember, on the hill

2

That overlooks the Esk, a cottage stands;
The summer's sun invites the blue-bell there,
The honeysuckle and sweet eglantine :
Thy father, bounteously, on mine bestowed
That cot, to shelter his declining days.
Its hearth was gladdened by a maiden's smile,
The old man's heart was lightened by her love.
Throughout the day she earned the scanty meal,
At evening sang the merry border songs,
Until my aged sire forgot his years
And thought himself again a stalwart man,
Out on the chase or mingling in the fray.
Among our hills her sprightliness and grace,
Her gentle voice and sympathizing ways,
Won her the favor of each neighboring swain,
And in our lowly lot, esteemed, admired,
She moved a queen !   That maiden was my sister.
The moon that wanes as blaze the Beltane fires,
Beheld her happy, now beholds her grave.

M. of Max. I may not weep with thee a private sorrow.
  Why art thou here ?   Be brief.

Carn. Forgive my tears :
  A se'nnight since, that maid by ruffian hands
  Was from her father violently torn—
  God of the Universe had I been there !
  In vain his gray hairs pleaded for the child
  The palsied arm no longer could protect :
  The howling wolf is guiltless of the crime.

When next I saw her, she was cold and dead ;
Drowned in the Liddel where the rowan-tree
(Famed in the legend) overhangs the linn.
She, in her frenzy, thought the wave would hide
Her shame and sorrow from the unpitying world.

M. of Max. He cannot render back the life she took
With irreligious haste. By whom said'st thou ?

Carn. By merciless Liddesdale.

M. of Max. Impossible !

Carn. For vengeance turning hitherward I ran :
A blazoned shield betrayed me to his serfs—
Taken, and forced before the cruel lord,
Stubborn and mute I stood resolved to die
Rather than utter word. With sudden thought
His anger cooled : he offered me my life
If I would swear to serve him as a mute.
I swore: 'twas not for liberty to breathe,
But for delicious, exquisite revenge.

M. of Max. I am amazed. Reveal thy hidden purpose,
That I may know how desperate is thy rage.

Carn. The strong and noble may inflict such wrongs
The humble vassal will rise up in strength,
Despite his grade, an independent man ;
And, as in terror, all distinction level.
A peasant born I bear a prince's heart,
Fit to contend against the proudest lord.

M. of Max. I listen, sirrah—madly damn thyself.

Carn. Throughout the border his fair daughter's name

In each prayer is remembered; I resolved
(Oh, kill me not till I unlade my soul,)
That he, in kind, should feel my father's woe :
In her sweet face I saw my sister's smile—
My spirit melted instantly to pity.   [sealed.

M. of Max. For that unhallowed thought thy doom is

Carn. I care not for my life : 'tis in thy hands ;
But for thy sake and her's expose me not.

M. of Max. Speaking or mute thou art a living lie.

Carn. Could I preserve thy days and gladden her's,
One act of present vengeance were complete.
Trust in her fears : I know his headstrong will,
Heard him declare his mortal hate of thee,
And purpose to bestow her hand on Hume.
In mercy to thyself, not me, I pray
Be in his presence vigilant and wary.

M. of Max. Base-hearted slave!

Carn. Despise me as thou wilt,
But I implore thee, Master, credit all :
If on the morrow thy resolve still holds,   [me,
When thou hast seen and proved him, and proved
Kill me by inches.

M. of Max. Leave me, slave ; begone !

                              [*Exit* CARNEGIE.

'Tis past belief, and yet if true or false,
I stand in a dishonorable place
Unless I speak.   Just as my bounding heart
Was bent to learn a fate, his story held me

Against my judgment, rooted to the spot.
O, chance inopportune!   But what is best?
Postpone our meeting, or (at once) expose
This strange impostor?   There is none to counsel.
O, guide me Fate, and keep my honor clear,
For in this conflict I am sore perplexed.
Within his veins must slumber ancient blood:
For gentle nature, as we sometimes find,
Rises above all antecedents known,
And proves a dash of untraced noble stock,
Which seeks its place among exalted men.
But I must act: first I shall write my father,
Then seek the private audience to confess
Our mutual love.   Unwelcome news forewarns.

[*Exit.*

SCENE II.—*A Court of* LIDDEL CASTLE.   *Enter* LID-
DESDALE *and* CARNEGIE.

Liddes. They of the dream and legend prate? No more?
    Let the fools babble, I regard not them.
    Did not young Maxwell and my daughter meet
    Within the hour alone?
Carn. Mabel and I
    Were present all the while.
Liddes. What heard'st him say?
Carn. Words that a lord might to a lady speak
    In manly courtesy.

Liddes. Thou low-born cur!
      Presumest thou to judge !   Sirrah, what words ?

Carn. He praised her needle that adorns the walls,
      Extolled her music that delights the ear ;
      And said her charming skill repays its toil
      With sweet perfection; then, to me they turned,
      And thanked their stars that they were blessed
                        [with speech.

Liddes. Spoke he not tenderly? Nor looked? Art true ?
      Nor sighed as if he would impress her heart ?
      What, not ?   Do none suspect thy counterfeit ?

Carn. I am thy slave—kill me, but doubt me not.

Liddes. I would, did not the prospect of thy service
      Outweigh my doubt.   If once discovered false,
      Tortures—thou can'st not think of them—terrible,
      Will be thy certain doom.

Carn. My lord, I swore.

Liddes. Sirrah, I would read thy heart; hear'st? Look up.
      Beware !   What said they of the threatening times ?

Carn. My gentle mistress sighed and wished that peace
      Might bless the land, for she is sick of war.

Liddes. And Maxwell ?

Carn. Fear not justice, he replied,
      Enraged the king, and swore to unfurl his pennon,
      If thou would'st ask.   [dependers ?

Liddes. (*After a smile of contempt.*)   And what say my

Carn. They fret that weeks pass in ignoble sloth ;
      And as they meet around the teeming board,

Pray that the threatening of the allied kings
Be changed to deeds, for they are tired of ease.
Liddes. Brave hearts! soon shall they see their hottest
That eye of fire which shrinks not at my gaze, [fray.
Bespeaks a soul above his humble grade,
And makes me, while I doubt, resolved to trust.

[*Enter* HUME, LOCHWOOD *and* CESSFORD.

Faint is the hope, young friend, that I shall win
My daughter's free consent—at least by smiles.
Hume. I must in patience bear her gentle scorn.
Loch. Well said, sir—like a lamentable lover.
Liddes. Her father's wish—decidedly expressed,
She dares not disobey. So far I spoke
Merely by hints to prove how she inclines:
But she affected not to understand.
Hume. I shall be ruled by thee and live in hope.
Loch. A maiden's heart is flexible—she will change,
My word on that, to gratify her father.
Grant that she Maxwell loves—it may be so—
She never said, that I have heard, she does.
My lord commands she must not think of him;
She weeps a sea of tears and sighs a tempest,
And vows she never will love man again.
Oh sir! I have known women do as much,
And in a month have married with another,
And loved him dreadfully. Women are—women!
Liddes. I promise thee; and for her dower I give

(When heaven calls me away) my wide domains,
Which, in her right defend, until a son
Blesses your loves and reaches manhood's years:
With them, let him inherit too my name—
For I must live on Scotland's page.   Scotia!
Land of my home and heart !   Dost thou consent ?

Hume. Gladly ; she mine, then am I truly blessed.
And for her jointure hereby I reserve
The full revenue of my lands in Merse.
In token of my reverence, all my power
I place at thy command, with this condition—
That I shall lead them where they march or fight.

Liddes. I am content : soon shall the clerk engross
The full particulars of this solemn league.
My daughter ! thee, an infant in these arms
I fondly clasped, and while you daily twined
Around my widowed heart, believed thee mine,
Nor ever dreamed that thou would'st be another's !
I am awake, and find in nature's course,
Another will enfold thee to his bosom
As I did thy sweet mother.   I shall be
Henceforth a sharer merely of thy love,
And mine the less—the greater is thy lord's.
When you become a father, sir, and feel
A father's love, no longer will you wonder
How sadness mingles in the hour of joy
Which sees a daughter wedded.   In giving her,
I give what dearer is than wealth or power,

The fairest, only blossom of my home!
As I have ever watched her gentle thoughts,
And each, as found, indulged; be thou to her
Tender and true—she is indeed the like—
Yielding and young. A comfort she will be,
A blessing to thy house, a sunbeam there,
To glad and gild thy heritage and name!

Hume. I feel—too much to speak.

              [*Enter* KENNETH.

Liddes. Well, sir, thy news.

Ken. The warder from the southern tower espies
A Herald riding hitherward.

Liddes. Admit him.   [*Exit* KENNETH.]

    As I surmised, my lords; we know not yet
If from the Wardens or the King he comes.
Soon shall we learn what they vouchsafe to tell;
Valiant in words no doubt: but we shall hear.

           [*Enter* MASTER OF MAXWELL.

Carn. Lost, lost! [*Aside.*]

M. of Max. If your kind grace——

Liddes. Sir, I am busy.

    I have no patience, he offends my sight.

              [*Aside to* HUME.

    Know'st thou a Herald comes?   [*To* MAXWELL.]

M. of Max. I hear you say so.

Liddes. Say! he is at the gate. Thou wilt excuse me.
    Dost guess his errand?

M. of Max. My lord, I do not know.

   2*

But I have come to crave, when leisure serves,
A single word in private.

Liddes. Well—content.   [in hope.

Carn. [*Aside.*] That look has cheered me, and I breathe

Liddes. Know'st thou the rowan-tree by Liddel's stream,
Where boldly rise the banks to overlook
The tumbling linn—a wild, secluded spot?

M. of Max. My lord, I do.

Liddes. There, as the weary sun
Kisses the hills and bids the world good-night,
Meet me—alone.

M. of Max. I shall not fail the time. [*Exit.*]

Liddes. This Herald cometh—he will speak of her—
But I shall mar his hope.   This Herald, friends—
                    [*Enter* KENNETH *and a Herald.*

Herald. By royal seal the Wardens held a Court,
At which indisputable proof was brought——

Liddes. One doubt is solved.   Come, sir, at once thy
message.

Herald. Of deeds illegal and high crimes committed,
By thee, the Lord of Liddesdale.

Liddes. Well, sir ?

Herald. I come not to enumerate the deeds
Of which thou art accused, but to declare
They have resolved to stop thy lawless course,
To bring thyself, thy kinsmen and dependers
To strict and fearful justice.

Liddes. Let them dare !

Herald. Yet with a generous spirit have agreed,
    (Ere they in power o'er-run this rebel land
    And deluge it with blood) to summon thee
    Before their Court; which, in their name I do—
    Thy oath of fealty they will accept,
    Then grant free pardon for offences past.
    If humbly thou dost acquiesce, I name
    Wednesday at noon the time, Carlisle the place.

Liddes. Aye, at the Haribee !   Am I a vassal ?
    Do they suppose that like a common felon
    I will appear and trembling beg their mercy ?
    Or like a pious, poor, priest-ridden knight,
    Confess my sins and pray to be absolved ?
    No, sir Herald, never !   Go, thou art safe:
    But had the best in person spoken thus,
    I would have cloven him from crown to nave.

Herald. So speak the Wardens.   And I am commis-
    To offer thee safe conduct hence and back, [sioned
    Which in these letters-patent is confirmed.

Liddes. Their letters-patent !   Herald, speak again—
    Send me safe conduct—me !   Presuming lords !
    By this uplifted sword to heaven I swear,
    My only safeguard is this sturdy brand,
    And true friends here.   Thy office I respect ;
    But they shall rue this insolence and scorn.

Herald. My lord, I wait thy answer.

Liddes. Answer—Go !
    Yet tell the haughty Wardens I deny

Their right to summon: tell them I despise
Their wondrous clemency and empty threats.
If they would see me—I am to be found.
Conduct the Herald to the outer gate.

> [*Exeunt* KENNETH *and Herald.*

Did not the Wardens tremble at my power,
Arms should pursue the heels of their intent,
Not braggart words.
Hume. What force is in the field ?
Liddes. Mine equals theirs—thanks to my brave allies.
Cess. Add double valor, discipline and skill,
  And we quadruple them.
Loch. Oh, well summed up !
Hume. Freely command; we are devoted, true.
Cess. Yea, unto death.
Liddes. I thank ye, noble friends.
  Soon shalt thou hear how well my pleading thrives.

> [*Exeunt* LORD HUME, CESSFORD *and* LOCHWOOD.

Go, sirrah, to thy mistress, and express
As best you may, by signs, I crave her presence.

> [*Exit* CARNEGIE.

Three hundred score are mine—securely mine—
A strong addition to my former power :
Thanks, natal star ! Wardens and Kings beware
How ye dispute my claims or slur my name.
Now to my child; heaven grant that gentle means
Incline her mind aright—or, should she prove

Unyielding to my hope, may no harsh word,
Nor deed of blood enforce my solemn promise.

[*Exit.*

SCENE III.—*An apartment in* LIDDEL CASTLE.
LADY CHRISTINA, MABEL *attending.*

Lady C. How slowly creeps the lazy-footed hour!
Had he the speed abounding in my love
He would be here already.   Wherefore chide?
'Tis my impatience more than his delay,
Makes hours seem long that keep their equal pace.
I will be more myself, nor once surmise
My father is unkind.

[*Enter* KENNETH.

Ken. My gentle mistress,
Young Maxwell meets our chief at set of sun.
Lady C. Why not till sunset? that is long to wait.
Kenneth, did he seem pleased?
Ken. Yes, he seemed happy.
Lady C. Then am I happy too, and full of hope.

[*Enter* CARNEGIE : *by signs he informs* LADY
CHRISTINA *that* LIDDESDALE *will visit her.*

You mean that he will presently be here.
O, had'st thou voice to speak!   Would'st say my
And I am to await him?   I obey.   [father,
It may be of the Herald he will speak,
Perhaps of Maxwell : can it be of Hume?
But I shall welcome him, nor doubt his love.

[Enter LIDDESDALE.

Liddes. Thy sainted mother's only gift! she died,
God save her soul! when thou wert but a child,
And left in thee a copy of herself.
E'en as thou look'st, she looked, when first our loves
Grew to confession and our hearts were one.

Lady C. A gentle tutor and a tender father
Thou ever art; may heaven preserve my life
To recompense thy tenderness and care.

Liddes. Send thy attendants hence.

  [Exeunt KENNETH, CARNEGIE *and* MABEL.
My dearest child,
Till smiling on thine own thou can'st not feel
The proud, the anxious joy I feel in thee.
But oh, sad thought! we are alone on earth,
And when we die our house becomes extinct;
And this old castle, whose gray walls have laughed
At centuries of storm and bloody siege,
May never echo to its master's tread—
A stranger race may sit around its hearth!

Lady C. My own dear father teach me how to soothe
Thy troubled thoughts, and if my skill avail,
Thou never wilt be sad.

Liddes. My generous daughter!
(Quite unaware her infant days are past,
So fleetly runs the unregarded time!)
Thy willing aid encourages my hope,
And I am happy: thou art spared to bless me.

Ere nature in its course shall close my eyes,
I wish to see thee wedded to a lord
Who will protect thee when I am no more.
How art affected toward my gallant Hume?

Lady C. He is thy friend, and merits my respect.

Liddes. Would he reply so coldly to thy praise?
The bravest, noblest of our Border Chiefs—
This day has he solicited thy hand.

Lady C. I never thought to look on him with love.

Liddes. What more could lady ask than he can give?
Wealth, title, power, affection and renown!

Lady C. But what avails this out-door world's applause,
With all the trappings wealth and honor bring,
If the poor heart sits comfortless at home?

Liddes. He is my friend—esteemed—has promised aid,
Which, in these stirring times, my need requires.

Lady C. Love, duty, honor—all that I may offer,
Would poorly pay thy never ceasing care,
And what a daughter has to give, I give—
Thine own to keep, not give away again.

Liddes. My sportive child! I knew thy yielding mind,
And promised him thy hand. Why! what! recoilest?

Lady C. Father to thee I owe a daughter's love.

Liddes. Add, obedience.

Lady C. Yes, obedience
In all where it is duty to obey.
By the remembrance of departed days,
By her who in their sunshine blest us both,

By sweet religion that subdues the world—
Yea, by yon heaven we fervently adore
And hope to gain, entreat me not to wed
Where not a thought is kindred with us twain.

Liddes. He has my promise—that I never broke.

Lady C. For a rash vow, wilt thou, like Israel's judge,
Thy own, thy only daughter sacrifice?
There is more honor in a promise broken,
If unadvised, than in that promise kept.

Liddes. I am thy source of life——

Lady C. Take then my life,
But do not take the affections of the soul
By heaven, not thee, bestowed. A curious art
May imitate the flower, which to the eye
At distance, seems as new-plucked from the stem,
But where's the perfume? God alone gives that!

Liddes. Men are alike, tho' woman's wayward fancy
Fashions this man an angel, that a fiend.
Your love invests some weak-armed foe of mine
With noble attributes, and for his sake
Would risk my present, and your future hope.
Be not so frail in duty—foolish, fond;
As, for the vain conceit he has inflamed,
To lose a father's and a husband's favor.
No answer! What, receive I no reply?
Through thee I form alliance with a chief
Who never turned his back on friend or foe—
One whose great aid my policy must win.

Lady C. False is the policy that is not just.

Liddes. Ha! rebel girl! art not afraid?　Beware!

Lady C. Why should I sacrifice a life's content
　　To meet a pressing object of the hour,
　　Which, with the hour, is past; or why commit
　　A certain wrong to reap uncertain good?

Liddes. My mandate issued is a border law
　　No soul can change, no sophistry evade.

Lady C. Father, forgive—this unexpected rage
　　Has chilled my blood and almost turned my brain;
　　I know not what I say.

Liddes. Dost thou relent?

Lady C. Father, dear father—humbly on my knees,
　　I pray thee, do not drive me to despair;
　　I am thy child, obedient save in this;
　　Yea, I will waste the richness of my youth
　　In fruitless maidenhood: I will do all,
　　Whate'er you ask unmurmuringly, save this.

Liddes. My word is sacred tho' the mountains fall.
　　A youth of fame—a husband for a queen!

Lady C. By mother's sacred memory, I pray—
　　Look on that picture, it is hers—so like
　　That cunning art has emulated life;
　　Move as I may, her eyes still turn on me
　　With an approving smile.　Lo you, behold!
　　The very canvas breathes!　Oh, Christ, it stirs!
　　Her voice is in my ears—she cries, hold, hold!
　　Oh blessed virgin, my dead mother's looks

I shall obey, and not a living sire !

Liddes. Illusion all ! This shallow, vain device,
 Will not prevail. Beware of disobedience,
 It was the first, the great unpardoned sin—
 For which man still endures the wrath of heaven.
 Thou art affianced—he is here to wed—
 Thy hand is his, whoever has thy love.

Lady C. No, by the Holy-rood, never !

Liddes. Never !
 If one alive has stolen thy heart from me,
 And taught this stubborn and unfilial spirit,
 Woe fall upon his life !

Lady C. Away disguise !
 Where I adore I fear not to confess :
 My troth is pledged to Maxwell ; I am his,
 He mine, and him I'll wed or none.

Liddes. Patience!
 Have I, like the fool in the fable, warmed
 A serpent in my bosom ?

Lady C. No power, no threat
 Shall move the firm foundation of my love,
 Nor shake my truth. Mother in heaven, hear!
 And, as I keep my vow, in thy good time
 Accept me, or reject me evermore!   [beware!

Liddes. Ingrate, thou knowest me ; as thou know'st,
 For thou hast seen when I have marched in wrath,
 That neither sex nor age, nor prayer nor wail,
 Sated my thirst for blood. I say, beware—

To thee I give one day to be resolved—
Wert not my child, denial were thy death.

Lady. C. Better to die than, linked with one unloved,
To bear through life each day a lingering death.
Were I to act unworthy of thy child,
Or of my sex, I should avoid thy gaze—
Yea, shun the blessed air, the light of day,
To seek companionship with toads and owls,
And never lift my voice aloud in prayer.

Liddes. Stay not to vex me, but resolve—away !

                       [*Exit* LADY CHRISTINA.

High soars the eagle with a noiseless flight,
While meaner birds scream loud on feeble wing :
May this hand wither if I slay him not.
Good warrant have I for his taking off—
On false pretences comes he to my castle
And steals a daughter's love, in league the while
With her own father's foes.   Before yon sun
Sinks in the drowsy west, the deed is done.
Heaven will behold and justify the blow
That stops a traitor's pestilential breath.   [*Exit.*

ACT III.

SCENE I.—*The Rowan Tree. A romantic spot; the river*
   LIDDEL *falls over a rocky precipice into a deep linn.*
   Enter MASTER OF MAXWELL *and Retainers.*

M. of Max. This letter give into lord Maxwell's hand;
   I charge thee rather lose thy life than this.
   Now, with thy fellows, home with swiftest speed.
   Away !   [*Exeunt Retainers.*
          As friends, alone we meet : how part ?
   A sudden gloom o'erspreads the face of nature—
   Yea, while I look, black clouds on clouds arise
   Like giants trooping on in fierce array,
   And chase all beauty from the sky, so late
   One perfect glory in the gilded west.
   They meet, they mingle ! From the conflict, see !
   The lightning glares—and hark! the thunder booms
   In mountain volleys from the airy steep.
   Down pours the rain, as if to drown a world,
   While howls the wind among the budding boughs,
   Which shake and groan 'neath the terrific blast.
   Heaven grant 'tis not prophetic of my fate !
   She is alone in all this dreadful coil,
   And chiding my delay.

Liddes. [*Without.*] Abide thou here ;
    Approach not till I call.

M. of Max. His voice ! how changed !
              [*Enter* LIDDESDALE.

Liddes. For once we meet befitting my intents—
    In nature's rage : hark to the elements !
    They harmonize with my awakened wrath
    And prophesy a doom.

M. of Max. What means my lord ?
    I freely tasted of thy generous cup ;
    On thy domain by invitation stand,
    And should be safe from rage or disrespect.

Liddes. By me unbidden cam'st thou here to-day,
    And this appointment is thy own, not mine :
    Thy subtle argument thus loses force
    And thou art self-convicted.

M. of Max. Speak my lord—
    Wherein have I offended ? Prithee speak.

Liddes. Dissembler ! inward turn thine eyes, survey
    Thy guilty soul and pluck the treason thence—
    For recent acts bear witness 'gainst thy words.

M. of Max. Bring me the man who dares asperse my name,
    And I will prove before thy face and heaven's,
    The monstrous lie.

Liddes. He stands before thee, sir !
    Thou art a traitor to my castle's cheer,
    And to its peace : against my honor leagued
    With royal foes, a villain and a spy.

M. of Max. Thou my accuser! Thou! then on my word—
        My simple word, thou art abused, my lord.
        None in the Border truer is than I,
        Or more devoted to thy ancient house.

Liddes. 'Tis false: thy father joins the Wardens' council;
        Thou, yesterday, wast there—to-day art here
        To pry into my plans, compute my power,
        And make report, where vantage may be gained.

M. of Max. Not so, not so ; on honest mission bent,
        I sought this meeting to declare a truth,
        And beg thy favor.

Liddes. Well, confess: speak out !
        The lying tongue convicts the guilty heart,
        For like two thieves they never tell one tale.

M. of Max. Tho' thou art roused to most unusual rage,
        Conscious of right, I fear not to avow—
        I love thy daughter, am by her beloved ;
        Abate thy wrath, with her consent I come
        To crave a father's blessing on us both.

Liddes. A fool once shot his arrow at the moon !
        What, win her ere I gave consent to woo ?
        Come to my castle like the midnight robber,
        To steal the richest jewel it contains,
        And then, confessing, beg it as a gift.   [late

M. of Max. One shelters 'neath thy roof, to whom of
        Some kindness I have shown—thy hate he knew,
        Advised me, when we met, to come prepared:

But I, confiding in thy noble soul,
Believed him not, but checked him and reproved.

Liddes. Insolent youth ! durst to my face confess
That thou hast tampered with a vassal's faith,
And won him with a bribe ?   Art thou prepared ?

M. of Max. My lord, my lord—a single word may save
A sea of blood.

Liddes. If thou hast courage, draw—
Or like a beggar die.

M. of Max. Compel me not
To strike against thy life—but pick thy best,
Yea, choose a thousand score, and I will prove
My faith and honor while the world looks on !

Liddes. No, not so witless to be thus entrapped
In such a flimsy snare.   Thou would'st gain time,
And therewith intercessors, or, slave-like,
Would'st seek an opportunity of flight ;
This mean device accelerates thy fate.
No boasting—prove !

M. of Max. Oh, speak, my honored lord—
Is there no way to mitigate thy rage ?

Liddes. Vain fool ! if not beyond redemption damned,
Pray for thy sins' remission : thou art doomed !

> [*They fight : a pause.*

M. of Max. I fight defensive.

Liddes. Thou must kill, or die.

M. of Max. O God !   I dare not take her father's life !

Liddes. No time to lose; prepare!   The daylight fades.

Wert thou of meaner birth a vassal's sword,
Not mine, should shed thy blood: that's some
The last that I will pay.   [respect,

M. of Max. Would 'twere a king !

              [*Exeunt fighting.*

     [*Enter* CARNEGIE.

Carn. God of the Universe, had I a weapon !
Steal not, O Ruin, like a wasteful thief,
A precious gem to hide it in the earth!
Shut down, O Night, the eyes of melting day,
And part the combatants. Brave youth, well fought.
Pity still lives on earth, and rules in heaven.
O Justice, be not blind ! But if he fall!
A strange device is gathering in my brain—
For Maxwell slain and my dear sister lost,
Let them in torments live, in terror die.

                 [*Exit.*

SCENE II.—*Night: a tapestried chamber in* LIDDEL
     CASTLE.   *Enter* LADY CHRISTINA : MABEL *and*
     KENNETH *attending.*

Lady C. He surely should return. Look out, good
I do forget 'tis night and pitchy dark. [Mabel—
The hag's prediction flashes on my mind ;
At eighteen years—that age I reach to-day—
A sad, a melancholy change, she said
Would overcloud the future of my life.

A thoughtless, gay and laughing damsel then,
I chid the crone and smiled at her prediction;
Then glared she on me with malignant eye,
And hummed the legend with her croaking voice—

> When cruel might
> Down-crushes right:
> When humble foes
> And high oppose,
> Listen the wail
> Of Liddesdale!

It seems like truth!   He comes! no, 'tis the storm.
Imagination might. with little stretch,
Liken the wind to groans, the rain to blood
Of wounded nature.

Mab. Woe is me, my lady!

Lady C. It is a night to please unhallowed sprites,
And drive men's brains to desperate rage or crime.
Good, guard the good!

         [*A Voice behind the arras.*

Voice. Lady of Liddesdale!

Lady C. Holy St. Mary!

Mab. May heaven preserve us, Kenneth! what is that?

Voice. Lady of Liddesdale!

Lady C. That voice again!

Mab. Kenneth, it is a Spirit; pray, oh pray!

Ken. I touch my beads, but cannot tell for fear.

Mab. In mercy lady, answer not a Sprite:
Kenneth, it is not safe.   Where shall we hide?

         [*Exeunt* KENNETH *and* MABEL *in terror.*

Voice. Lady of Liddesdale !

Lady C. Thrice am I named !

    Where have the timid fled? What would'st, Unseen?

Voice. This morn the sun dawned on thy natal day :

    Gone is his glory—then lament the past.

Lady C. The past, the past ! tell me the coming doom.

    If, Unseen one, thou art a Spirit of light,

    No mockery—not from the evil pit,

    Thy far fore-seeing eye can look beyond

    The laggard hour, and read the great events

    May shake the world with fear.   Reveal to me

    The purpose of thy visit.   If thou com'st

    To teach me how I better may fulfil

    My duty as a Christian and a daughter

    Than my frail, sinful heart has present power,

    Listening, in meek submission I'll obey.

Voice. The past, the past—

Lady C. Declare the present truth.

Voice. To thee and thine, woe, ceaseless woe.

Lady C. Mercy !   [when—how ?

    Woe, ceaseless woe !   To whom ?   Speak—what—

Voice. Master of Maxwell !

Lady C. Gracious heaven !

Voice. Thy father !

Lady C. Thee I adjure, Unseen, by him thou servest,

    And by this Cross, dear emblem of my faith,

    Give me to know—reveal the will of heaven !

Voice. Behold ! they part beneath the rowan-tree,

The face of one is like its blossom, pale :
The other's sword is like its berry, red !

Lady C. Holy Virgin ! Thou dreadful riddler, speak !

Voice. Go read the mystery 'neath the withered leaves.

Lady C. I will !

Where art thou, nurse ? Maxwell or father,
I dare not choose. Does frenzy rule my brain ?
Is this unreal—a dream ? Live I, and hear ?
Has heaven vouchsafed to warn me of my fate,
And made me strong to bear it ; or am I
`Selected as its instrument. to keep
The hand unred and prove the legend false?
By thy dear memory, mother, sainted one!
I pray for daring greater than my years
And sex possess ! Come, Mabel ; Kenneth, come :
Hide ye in fear ? Would to the limbs of age
We could give speed, and courage to the heart.

     [*Re-enter* MABEL *and* KENNETH.

Quick light our torches, quick !

Mab. Alas, my lady !

Lady C. Thy torches, quick !

Ken. She is bewitched !

Lady C. Obey.

Though the earth trembles at this dreadful tale,
I feel no storm, but here. Come quickly, follow.

       [*Exeunt.*

  [CARNEGIE *comes from his place of concealment.*

Carn. At length my hour of vengeance dawns, fit time

When earth affrighted bellows forth revenge!
My great device is only half performed ;
I will escape and reach the fatal tree ;
And there command a deed so strange and wild,
She, in her frenzy, will believe divine.   [*Exit.*

SCENE III.—*Night: a wild and rugged scene.   Thunder and lightning.   Enter* LADY CHRISTINA, MABEL
and KENNETH *following.*

Ken. Our torches are blown out.
Mab. Be not afraid.
Ken. I do not fear the man that sees with eyes
    And works with hands.   Preserve me from ill
        Sprites.
Mab. She hath not spoken, Kenneth ; not a word ;
    Nor wept a tear—sure sign she is bewitched.
Ken. Would, Mabel, I could soundly beat the hag,
    No power would she have then to harm our lady.
            [*The lightning strikes a tree.*
Lady C. Mercy ! the lightning blasts our crested Pine.
Ken. I live by breath and bread, and am afraid.
Lady C. Shielder of virtue ! guide my steps aright—
    Where stands the rowan-tree ?
Mab. Courage Kenneth—
    No Witch dares venture near a rowan-tree.
        [CARNEGIE *from his place of concealment.*
Carn. Lady of Liddesdale, here !
Lady C. That voice again !

Mab. Save me, Kenneth; oh! save my lady too.

Ken. You're wiser, Mabel, and may lay the Sprite.

Mab. You are a man.

Ken. I never was at Padua—

    What can I do against the Powers of Darkness?

Lady C. Spirit of good or evil, I approach

    Obedient to thy summons: teach me where

    The mystery lies.

Carn. Lady of Liddesdale, here!

Mab. It cannot be a Spirit; it spoke first.

Ken. Trust not the evil one.

Lady C. And I am here!

Carn. Come, read the truth beneath the withered leaves.

Lady C. The withered leaves! withered! Where is the

Mab. On yonder cliff that overhangs the linn.   [tree?

Ken. Is it not a Kelpie?

Mab. Where is its light?

Ken. Do Kelpies speak?

Mab. All comes in time ordained!

Lady C. Should evil things speak of the evergreen,

    Or come so near the living, leaping stream!

    I breathe in hope: 'tis but a step, and then—

                            [*Exeunt.*

SCENE IV.—CARLISLE: *morning. The Wardens'*
Court. SIR JOHN CHARTERS *and* WM. LORD DACRE.
Their huge chairs decorated with the arms of their
respective kingdoms.   Officers attending.   Lords,
Heralds, Mosstroopers, Peasants, etc.

Sir John Ch. " If they would see me I am to be found."
　　Were these his words, and in defiant tone ?
　　We'll hear no cause to-day: let all depart.
　　　　　　　　[Exeunt Mosstroopers, Peasants, etc.
　　Presumptuous lord, thou yet shalt rue this scorn !
Lord D. Most insolent and bold : alike insulting
　　Both to our royal masters and ourselves.
　　A sharp reply should instantly be sent,
　　Not in vain words—let our sharp weapons speak it.
Sir John Ch. Death to the rebel ! death !
Lord D. Permit one chief
　　To live rebellious to his sovereign lord,
　　Why not a score, why not a hundred score?
　　The rounded crown were then an infant's toy ;
　　The sceptre but a wand for children's sport ;
　　The globe a ball for men to play at games,
　　And all authority and law reviled.
Sir John Ch. One course, and one alone remains for us,
　　Which courage prompts and loyalty demands.
Lord D. Emboldened in the time of Regent's rule,
　　(Never before did woman rule in Scotland)

He thinks thy king, a justice-loving prince,
Will still permit disloyal knaves to thrive
On plunder wrung from unoffending men.
Sir John Ch. On every station light the beacon fires,
That loyal hearts may muster for the fight.
Ride to Dunfermline with the latest news.

> [*Exit a Herald.*

With those, though few, now quartered at Carlisle,
We march without unnecessary stop.
At Langholm we shall meet the northern lords
Prepared for forty days.

> [*Enter* LORD MAXWELL.

> Thou art right welcome.

Years overtask thy strength : I pray thee, sit.
Lord Max. I have, perhaps should say I had, a son—
They tell me that an old man's heart is cold
And all his feelings blunted : I deny it—
Witness these tears. But read and learn the cause.

> [*He gives* SIR JOHN CHARTERS *a letter.*

Sir John Ch. [*Reads.*]

> " My honored father: I write not in absolute danger,
> but under warning of a coming ill. In the service of
> Lord Liddesdale, whose guest I am, is Carnegie, thy
> vassal, feigning a mute and thirsting for revenge on the
> betrayer of his sister. If the story of his wrongs be
> true, so may his warning. Though humble born, there
> is a nobility in his soul worthy of remembrance. If I
> am alive, expect me to-morrow noon: if I return not,
> seek me. Take to thy heart my pleasantest thoughts.
> Adieu."

What means thy son?   Believe me, he is safe.

Lord Max. Why is he slain, and I, an old man, spared ?
      In nature's course he should my eye-lids close.

Lord D. Thy fear o'erleaps the green-strewn path of
      And in the quicksands of despair sinks down. [hope,
      A thousand chances may detain him hence,
      And still in safety.

Sir John Ch. Who is Carnegie ?

Lord Max. Son to a man whose years outnumber mine;
      A good one in his day.   To glad his age
      I gave him free a cottage by the Esk,
      Where dwelt he with an only son and daughter.
      The young man's heart is cast in nobler mould
      Than commonly is found in peasant life—
      'Tis said he wore a caul when he was born.
      The maiden walked the hills with queen-like grace,
      Like one of gentle birth, till, basely wronged,
      She drowned herself—preferring death to shame.
      Since then the brother has been missed from home ;
      Whither he went, this letter first reveals,
      And all confirms the danger of my son.

Lord D. Danger, my lord ! thine lives but in surmise.

Lord Max. Forgive my grief; bear with me for the sake
      Of this snow-covered head and wintry heart.
      In all his life he never caused a tear ;
      Now, in his death, my tears like rivers run.

Sir John Ch. We promise, save in duty to our king,
      To aid thy son, if not beyond relief.

Lord Max. But yesterday a lover went he forth
    With hope elate—but I will not digress :
    My mind still wanders—'tis the old man's plague.
    Perhaps he languishes in loathsome cell—
    I would restore him to the blessed light :
    Perhaps is slain—I would redeem his corse,
    That it may rest in consecrated ground.
    Oh, hear me, lords, turn from your present purpose;
    Seek Liddesdale in peace, and he may grant
    To you, what to the Herald he denied :
    Which proved, a bloodless victory is won,
    And I may find great consolation yet.

Sir John Ch. What think'st?

Lord D. There is some force in his suggestion ;
    But more to grant this worthy chief's request
    Than in the hope of vantage, I advise.
    If we should fail, more wisdom lines our cause,
    And thy young king, for patience, justice, truth,
    Already famous, will applaud the act.

Sir John Ch. Heralds attend, and officers of court,
    With all the Wardens' guard of horse and foot,
    We shall at once set out in proud array.
    Sound the trumpets.

Lord D. There's much in pomp and show
    To awe the humble and amaze the proud.

                          [*Exeunt.*

SCENE V.—*Morning: the Tapestried Chamber.* LADY
　　CHRISTINA *seated.* MABEL *and* KENNETH *attending.*

Lady C. If it be true the terrible tale is told,
　　And our proud name shall henceforth be erased
　　From Scotland's page.　Oh, cruel, bloody deed !
　　My soul recoils with horror from the thought,
　　Yet fate decrees it !　Sainted mother, rest:
　　Implore his pardon at the mercy-seat,
　　If it be true—he needs thy pleading there !
Mab. She has not closed her eyes the livelong night :
　　If she could weep 'twould be a sweet relief.
Ken. It is a miracle.
Mab. Heaven's will be done !
Ken. How heavy are the dead—the murdered dead !
Mab. Oh, Kenneth, what a sigh !　Her heart will break.
Ken. Hush, Mabel, hush! she charged us both to silence.
　　　　　　　　[*Enter* LIDDESDALE.
Liddes. Why, daughter, wear'st thou such unwonted
　　looks ?
　　Thine aspect frights me more than all my enemies.
　　Say, what is this ?　No answer!　Daughter speak ?
　　What know you, Mabel ?　Kenneth ?　Silent all !
Lady C. Father !
Liddes. Thy mother's image : speak again—
　　Thy voice delights me—mournful tho' it sounds.
　　Look up, my child, and wear a brighter face.

Lady C. I ever loved thee—was obedient ever.

Liddes. Save once—have I not been to thee a father.

Lady C. Save only once—Oh, would I could forget!

Liddes. Hast thou relented yesterday's resolve
　　And wish to say a father shall be pleased?
　　Then say it with a cheerful look and tone,
　　And not with one so sad.

Lady C. Sad though I seem,
　　There is no sorrow here—'tis gone forever:
　　There is no feeling here—'tis turned to stone. [say?

Liddes. Thy looks distress me, child: what would'st thou,

Lady C. To show thee sculpture by a master hand,
　　So life-like, wanting only breath to speak.

Liddes. Sculpture! Well, go on: I listen patiently.

Lady C. A piece of curious and excelling art,
　　No mortal's chisel ever shaped the like;
　　A warrior brought it from the Holy Land,
　　And by Our Lady vowed it should be mine.
　　It is; and here. In that recess it stands:
　　Till thou advise where is its fittest place,
　　'Tis hid behind the arras.

Liddes. This is strange—
　　What, sculpture from the land to which of yore
　　The royal Bruce's heart was borne, and where
　　The precious blood of Scots like rivers ran
　　For the redemption of the sacred tomb
　　From the blaspheming Infidel! Sculpture!

Without my knowledge how was it obtained,
From whom, and when?

Lady C. Where shall the marble stand?

Liddes. Remove the curtain and I will decide.

Lady C. Remove it, sir, thyself.

Liddes. Let us behold it!

> [LIDDESDALE *withdraws the arras; the body*
> *of* MASTER OF MAXWELL *discovered.*

Lady C. Look and declare—is't sculpture, as I said?

Liddes. What damned devil prompted this deceit?
Why show it thus? Think'st thou I joy to see
The corse of him whom living I despised?
This carcase better would become a pit
Than taint my castle with its noisome fumes.
Hence with it to the crows, the wolves, or waves!
Who, daughter, did this deed?

Lady C. What deed? Ask you?

Liddes. Yea, answer me: how came this body here,
By what foul means—by what insane device?

Lady C. By holy means! By superhuman aid!
And I, selected by the grace of heaven
Its agent stand, empowered to question thee.

Liddes. Is this my child, and these her old domestics?
Am I myself? Why, daughter, darest thou
With false and frenzied speech address me thus?

Lady C. I am commissioned by a power divine,
From whose all-searching eye there's nothing hid;
He sees the gem deep in the undelved mine;

All, earth con ns—the pearl in ocean's depths—
Thy secret heart and all its laboring thoughts,
As plainly as we see the wondrous sun
Blazing above the clouds.
Liddes. This is a marvel :
    Has she communion with the better world !
    I will not question now ; perhaps, to-morrow.
Lady C. Stay, sir! As vengeance rests with heaven
      alone,
    Speak, answer my demand : sculpture or death ?
Liddes. Death, daughter, death !
Lady C. Know'st thou the murderer ?
Liddes. Were it not for thy wild and haggard look,
    I would severely, yea, in anger chide thee ;
    But, as some evil power hath turned thy brain
    To desperate thought, I pity, not condemn—
    Look to your mistress.
Lady C. Go not ! Touch the corse.
Liddes. Daughter, wherefore ?
Lady C. Assure me it is death—
    I saw him yesterday in manly strength,
    With love elate and honor heart-full fraught,
    With every attribute of joyous youth,
    He seemed more like an angel than a man,
    And won the admiration of the world.
    How should a change so horrible as this
    Be in an instant real ? Touch the corse !
Liddes. Did ever child o'erawe a father ? Wherefore ?

Lady C. If at thy touch blood gushes not afresh,
    A silent, weeping witness 'gainst the hand,
    Then art thou guiltless of this dreadful deed,
    And the mysterious One a fiend of hell.
             [CARNEGIE *from his place of concealment.*

Carn. Haughty Lord of Liddesdale
    Touch the corse so cold and pale.

Liddes. What voice is that ?   My hand is on his heart !

Lady C. Blood ! blood !   O Christ, his hand is stained
    with blood !
    Come Mabel, Kenneth—see his gory hand,
    And testify the truth to all the world.
    Unnatural father !   Thou did'st murder him.
    Forewarned, I am the instrument of heaven
    To prove thy deed and prophesy thy doom !

Carn.   " Listen the wail
           Of Liddesdale ! "

Liddes. That voice again !   There is defiance still !
    And lo ! the blood still oozing from the wound
    Weeps for this wreck and melts my soul to pity.

Lady C. Thou dost confess the sacrilegious deed !

Liddes. Draw close the arras—hide him from my sight !

Lady C. Oh, good and holy Spirit, ere thy time
    Of righteous vengeance comes, subdue his heart ;
    Take him not off o'ertopped in innocent blood
    Unwailing, unatoning : make him feel
    The need of prayer and not too proud to pray
    Accept his penance and absolve his sins.

Liddes. Why, what is this? awake, firm heart, arouse!
    There's no revealment from the unknown realm.
    Did you connive at this? Who did? Speak out!
    Who was't informed her of the traitor's death?

Mab. I am a Christian hoping for salvation,
    It was a Spirit.

Ken. So indeed, my lord.

Liddes. Ignorant fools! Why did the arras rustle
    As if a palpable and living form,
    Not one of air, did stealthily pass behind?
    What! pale with fear; I shall myself, find out.

Lady C. Blest is the corse the rain rains on. Behold!
    The sudden shower attacks the window bars,
    Struggling to invade the chamber: it is past.
    Now smiles the sun upon that pallid face,
    Beautiful in death! Could'st thou abide with me
    Cold as thou art, no music from thy lips,
    No balmy breath, no sparkle in thine eyes—
    I could be happy lingering by thy bier;
    But 'tis forbid: Decay with withering touch
    Will blight the beauty death could not destroy.

Mab. Sweet lady, weep—weep or thy heart will break.

Liddes. Nothing is here, not seen. What, is this jug-

Lady C. As he was ever all the world to me,   [gling?
    So all, save breath, is lost in losing him.

Liddes. Remove the body: lead her to her chamber.
    He was a subtle traitor: I will answer
    To heaven and earth the justice of his death. [*Exit.*

Lady C. Ha! ha! ha! good, yes, good.   Come hither,
   Mabel—
   A thought, a plan, an excellent device!
   I'll do it: nurse, I will confide in thee!
                          [*Whispers to* MABEL.

Mab. Woe and alas for thy poor wits!
Lady C. Come on:
   Our torches, quick: what, hide ye both in fear?
   It is a blessed Sprite, no harm is near.
      By living stream and evergreen,
      Unhallowed, thou dar'st not be seen!
                          [*Exeunt.*

ACT IV.

SCENE I.—LIDDEL CASTLE. *Enter* LIDDESDALE, *a* PRIEST
and KENNETH.

Liddes. Quote not to me, O Priest, these common texts!
    Let superstitious fools believe in Fate,
    And quail beneath her inoracular voice—
    False lights mislead the brain of credulous men :
    I must have proof, or hold it phantasy.
Priest. That is irreverence!
Liddes. She is possessed!
    If thou can'st not this devil exorcise,
    That pales my heart and tyrannizes hers,
    Why, what avail the prayers of Holy Church ?
Priest. Thy good physician has exhausted art;
    Would he might cleanse her mind to hear the truths
    Of sweet religion !   On the brain distraught
    The Gospel word, like rain on sandy wastes,
    Falls barren down—no quickening grace is there.
Liddes. Mouth full of words !   Bring me the man sincere,
    Whose actions with his sacred office square,
    And I will give him reverence as a saint.
              [*Enter* MABEL.
How is your mistress, Mabel ?   Lo! she comes.

[*Enter* LADY CHRISTINA.

Lady C. But that will never be: Oh never more!

Mab. Sometimes she muses as you see her now;

     Again she smiles, but often sadly sings;

     Whiles, seeks for one she will not find, and asks

     If he is shriven and Christain burial had.

Liddes. Where is my Mute ?   Vile slave, let him appear

     And answer her.   To me, his use is past.

Lady C. They say a May-bride is a mourning bride,

     We shall not wed till June : nay, ask me not,

     For April is too soon.   And he consented !

     No danger threatens, love: lo you, behold !

     My sandals are not green.   I will not dance;

     Then, wherefore such a frown !   Nor shall I sing—

     A singing bride turns to a weeping wife.   [flower,

Liddes. Have trees no gum—have fields no herb nor

     The earth no mineral for mental ills—

     No virtue left in good Saint Fillan's well?

     Can my physician nothing more prescribe ?

     Is there no balm for the tormented brain?

Priest. From heaven alone, by prayer may come relief.

Lady C. Behold that gash !   O flinty-hearted man,

     And you stood by, nor raised an arm to save him !

Liddes. A sadder sight a father never saw.

Lady C. The steeds stand saddled at the Abbey gate,

     The solemn rite performed : they mount, they speed

     Fleet as the wind a-down the mountain gorge.

     Well done, proud roan, a better never paced !

See how he tosses high his haughty head
With flowing mane, and lightning-like he leaps!
What cloud is that?   The rider is o'erthrown
And dashed against the rocks!   Where is the horse?
The huge red sun, too heavy in his sphere,
Will fall and crush the world.

Priest. Her fancy runs
  To the old custom on a marriage-day.

Lady C. Last night the slipper prophesied his doom.
  Oh never will glad tidings reach her door;
  That bride can never thrive nor bless her lord:
  And wedded love shall never gladden more!

Priest. In vain I pray, and exorcism fails.

Liddes. If she could sleep!   Better to sleep forever
  Than thus to live.

        [*Enter* LORD HUME.

My lord, this was my daughter—
Would she could welcome thee.

Hume. A lovely wreck:
  This sight subdues my fondest aspirations.

Lady C. Sweet daisies bloomed a thousand years ago,
  They are not withered yet; and mountain brooks
  Still sing as blithely as they did of yore
  To listening rocks and trees; still, larks on wing,
  As stars retire, salute the awakening morn,
  And lovers wake in joy.   Why art thou sad?
  He did consent: I heard him.   Mabel, thou?

Hume. Can grace and beauty fall so very low!

Lady C. What say—shall we go gather hips and haws?

Liddes. The threat of kings, the loss of friends, all ills

Misfortune ever heaped upon my head—

Nothing has wrought such agony as this!   [now!

Priest. Ah, proud, stern lord, how art thou humbled

May good seed planted grow to harvest time

And yield an hundred fold.

Mab. Amen!

Lady C. Oh, oh!

[*Scarcely recognizes Hume, yet shrinks from him.*

Hume. Would I were hence.

Lady C. Oft as I looked a-field,

The ploughman in his furrow turned from me;

I said ill omen; but ye all cried, nay.

Tell me, whose judgment erred? Mine! Ha, ha, ha!

Liddes. She is not fitted for a bridal-bed.

Time, the great curer, may restore her wits,

And then, my lord—our royal foes advance;

To-morrow we shall have a busy day.

When we return triumphant from the war,

We may be welcomed with a smiling face—

And thy reward shall be her willing hand.

Lady C. Our torches, Mabel, quick!   No danger,
Kenneth,

Come, come—to living stream and evergreen.

[LADY C. *rushes out.*

Liddes. Follow your mistress, Mabel; watch her closely.

[*Exit* MABEL.

Hume. What cause—what dreadful cause?

Liddes. Young Maxwell's death.

Hume. Dead, dead!

Liddes. He was a traitor, and I slew him.

Hume. He was a gentleman of matchless worth.

Liddes. 'Twas justice prompted me, and not revenge.

Hume. Though in the list of honor stands my name
    Equal to thine, yet the respect I owe
    Less to thy rank than age, forbids rebuke.
    I held a promise Maxwell's life was safe.

Liddes. 'Tis false ; were she restored to pristine health,
    Repeat these words, and thou art instant doomed.

Priest. Relentless lord, will not the present anguish—
    The terrible picture in this house of sorrow—
    Suffice to quell thy spirit!   Prithee turn
    Thy thoughts from wrath and strife.   'Twere
      better far
    The treasures wasted in unnatural broils
    Were offered up in penance to the church.

Liddes. O selfish Priest ! Give, give ! the eternal theme.
                    [*Exit* Priest, *offended.*

    Thy speech, young man, o'ersteps thy rank and
      years;   [tongue.
    Awe, in my presence, should have checked thy
    Beware, I say; I have esteemed thee well :
    But, were my love capacious as the sky
    That clips the universal globe about,
    Utter these words again—it melts to air.

Hume. I came for welcome, not uncivil words.
    'Tis plain my power is all thy friendship prized;
    Her love I never had—thy promise only.
    Innocent instrument of wrong, I stand
    Without fit weapon to contend with thee,
    And so, farewell.

                            [*Exit.*

Liddes. He goes from me in anger:
    Insulting youth!   Go, call him back.   Stay, sir.
               [KENNETH *going—returns.*
    I never will solicit mortal aid:
    Let him pursue his course while I run mine.

                            [*Exeunt.*

SCENE II.—*An open country.* *A march: enter* SIR
    JOHN CHARTERS, LORD WM. DACRE, LORD MAX-
    WELL, *other Lords, Wardens' Guards, etc.*

Sir John Ch. Here halt awhile: our wearied troops
    require
    Both food and rest.   This is a lovely day—
    The air is mild, and blandly shines the sun,
    And not a trace of last night's storm remains.
Lord D. How far hence is his castle?
Sir John Ch. Some three miles.   [trees
    Look down yon wide-spread vale; there, 'mong the
    Round which the Liddel winds a devious course,
    His battlements are indistinctly seen.

Lord D. A pleasant landscape: here should peace abide,
  While war's wild havoc seeks a rougher scene.
  The hills are white with sheep, and in the valleys
  The cattle graze; on slopes the tillage smiles,
  And here and there I see the cottage home.
  The solemn stillness round, for thee, old Knight,
  Presages well: thy son shall bless thee yet.

Lord Max. Oh grant it, gracious heaven! in mercy
  Where is my son?   [grant!

          [*Enter* CARNEGIE, *breathless.*

Carn. My lord, he is at peace.

Lord Max. Tell me, in brief, how came he to his end?

Carn. By Liddesdale in single strife he fell.

Lord Max. An old man lingering on the verge of time,
  The nearer Thee, asks curses on his head.
  Oh strike him childless—may he pray for death,
  But nature do that great relief deny—
  Keep him alive, the wonder of the world!

Lord D. Our sorrow takes strange shapes and some-
      times wins
  Less sympathy than mirth: all men respect
  An unobtrusive grief.

Sir John Ch. Where is the corse?

Carn. For days his minions looked on me, a mute,
  Not feigned, but laboring under Nature's spite.
  Sorrow and rage in violent conflict joined,
  And broke my counterfeit. I spoke aloud!
  Declaring 'twas a Providence! They stood

Amazed, and asked, what miracle is this?
The murder of an innocent lord, I cried;
And, by the self-same Power that loosed my tongue,
I stand commissioned to protect his corse.
Quick bear it hence, convey it to his sire
For Christian burial in the ancestral vault.
Deeming me favored by the grace of heaven,
They, at my word, as a command divine,
In silent reverence bore the corse away.
Under my lead so far had they advanced,
(Beneath yon oak they've halted with the bier)
When I beheld your Banner on the hill,
And, breathless, I have come to speak this grief.

Lord Max. Only a father suffering loss like mine
May feel this agony—all others talk.
Did he defend himself?

Carn. Bravely, bravely!

Lord Max. A drop of comfort.

Sir John Ch. Thou art Carnegie!
No time have we to share this old man's sorrow,
Nor question thee.

Lord Max. Oh bear me to his bier;
There, kneeling, will my heart dissolve in tears.

Lord D. No longer parley with this treacherous lord,
His heart is steeled 'gainst nature, pity, justice;
And our forbearance but encouragement
To fouler crimes.   There's madness in his course,
A sure forerunner of his coming fall.

Sir John Ch. Altho' our march has been unprofitable,
    Which we lament—a worthy motive urged us,
    That merited success.
Lord Max. My brave, bright boy !
    A generous heart is cold—a purer soul
    Ne'er asked for mercy at the Eternal Gate.
Lord D. This man, whose bearing favors better blood
    Than flows in peasant veins, may give us aid,
    By knowledge of the rebel's plans and power.
Sir John Ch. When we have paid our duty to the dead,
    Invite him to our presence for his news.
    We must wipe out this plague-spot in the land.
Lord D. Once lose advantage, it is lost forever:
    Now is the surest time for deeds not dreams.
                         [*Exeunt.*

SCENE III.—*A wood: enter* CESSFORD *and* LOCHWOOD,
                  meeting.

Cess. More stirring news they tell me is abroad.
Loch. The king himself in arms?
Cess. I have not heard :
    But Hume has gone in haste, some say in dudgeon.
Loch. What is the matter with the love-sick youth?
    So busy was I brushing up my armor,
    I have not heard a whisper since we parted.
Cess. One of my friends while riding hitherward
    Met him, with all his followers, speeding north.

"Good morrow, whither bound so fast ?" quoth he;

"Where the road leadeth," was the brief reply.

Loch. Much information was not given in that.

Cess. One lagged behind the rest, vouchsafed to say

    That angry words had passed 'twixt two proud

        lords ;

    But what the discord, was beyond his guess.

Loch. If true, then is our right hand paralyzed.

Cess. Shall I, old friend, adventure on my guess ?

Loch. Ask me who never feared to speak aloud ?

Cess. Of will imperious, Liddesdale would make

    His thought the standard—like the knave of old—

    For each man's judgment; and as alien holds

    Whoever contradicts. To keep his favor,

    New service daily must we render him,

    And in the vein congenial to his mood,

    Or else we lose him.

Loch.   When discovered this ?

    At least you must confess in him one merit;

    He loves his daughter.

Cess. None will that deny;

    But even there his temper domineers.

Loch. Does Hume's desertion cool thy ardor, friend ?

Cess. I have not said he has deserted us,

    Nor if he had his course would alter mine.

    Yet, though subdued in manner, Hume still keeps

    Coals in his heart, that soon are blown to flame,

    And he's a-fire.

Loch.-Not fire of hate, but love
    Glows like the furnace, told in Holy Writ,
    That never singed a lock of three good men.
    I tell you love is stronger far than hate,
    That is, at twenty-five: had he my years,
    When blood has lost some of its molten heat,
    It might be different.   Think ye, for a word,
    That he would sacrifice so rich a jewel ?
    Pride against passion could not so rebel.
    We yet shall see the youth : my word on that.
Cess. I have known men who, for offended pride,
    In sullen mood bore tortures like the damned,
    And, in their suffering, thought they fed revenge.
Loch. Oh, well enough to preach; young blood a-fired
    With beauty, maelstrom-like, down swallows all.
          [Enter LIDDESDALE
Liddes. They are in earnest, and I am right glad,
    There is brave work to do.
Loch. What is the news ?   [guard,
Liddes. The northern lords have joined the Wardens'
    And hitherward they march.   Tho' Hume retires,
    Yea, were he more than neutral, I have friends
    To crush their vaunted power.
Loch. But what of Hume?
Liddes. My daughter is afflicted in her mind;
    Which, added to the Wardens' growing power,
    Emboldened him to speech that I rebuked :
    And he went hence in ill-concealed rage.

Cess. I must o'ertake him; if fair words prevail,
    He will return.
Liddes. Stay! Not at my request—
    I will not sue to him nor man alive.
Cess. But I may listen to his argument.
    Is there a hope she yet may be restored?
Liddes. There is.
Cess. What shall I say from thee?
Liddes. The truth.
    All I have said, report—not more: yes, add,
    My word is sacred tho' he gave offence;
    Her hand is his, when pristine days return,
    If he dare claim it: let his course decide.
Cess. I will o'ertake my friend.   [*Exit.*
Loch. Well, he is gone!
    I do not like his eagerness to go.
Liddes. Enticing from our foes who might be theirs,
    We doubly fortify ourselves.
Loch. Well said;
    But I will not believe the youth is false.
    Were it not wise with Hepburn to confer?
Liddes. Confer with him! No, he is weak in soul,
    And never helps a friend nor hurts a foe.
    We must confer with better, bolder men.
Loch. Refuse him not a chance to aid the right.
    If Hume deserts us, there is doubt of Cessford;
    Then, from the weakest we may need assistance.
Liddes. Thou art the truest, bluntest in the land;

A steadfast friend through twenty bustling years:
How few are spared to own so rich a treasure!
While thy old heart is true and full of blood,
Tho' selfish, craven men, like Hume, forsake
The holiest cause that ever called to arms—
The freedom of the lords against the king—
Never despair. Arouse new courage up:
Inspire with tenfold vigor every friend,
And make amends for false ones in our need.
Tho' signs of sadness hover in the air,
And tho' forebodings overcloud my brow,
Despite the worst, I'm eager for the fray.

                                                 [*Exeunt.*

SCENE IV.—*A chamber in* LIDDEL CASTLE. LADY
   CHRISTINA *reposing on a couch.* PRIEST, MABEL
   and KENNETH *attending.* *Ladies in waiting.*

Priest. It is not sleep. Her sands are nearly run:
   The pulse no more articulately beats,
   But simply flutters like an oil-spent lamp.
Mab. Where is the doctor? Is there no relief?
Priest. She's past all human aid; and I am here
   To pay the last sad office of the church:
   But unavailing is my holy power.
   O, heaven restore her, strengthen her to hear
   Words of salvation in her dying hour!
Ken. Grant, heaven, in mercy grant!

Mab. Dear, dear mistress.

    How changed that face, O Kenneth, sadly changed!

Priest. Pity her sunny days should set in gloom.

Mab. We never more shall hear her voice: never!

Priest. Thy will be done! Hush, hush, she stirs!

Lady C. [*Awakening slowly.*] Good nurse!

Mab. Would I could give my old life down for thine.

Lady C. Where am I? I have had a long, long sleep,

    And dreamed such dreams, glad am I to awake.

    Have I been sick? Oh, Mabel, I am weak;

    Help me. Kenneth! good old man. Who art thou?

Priest. Thy own confessor. God bless thee, lady!

Lady C. I dreamed the sun to darkness had returned,

    And my dear lover slain—speak, holy man!

Priest. Peace, peace!

Lady C. Open the window: give me air.

    And I will so beguile his angry heart

    He must consent: I yielded much to him.

    Join in our prayer, thy pleading will avail.

    Yes, beckon me; I come. Bring me my harp—

    With music I will meet the angelic choir.

            [*Motions as if playing on a harp,*

              and hums a plaintive melody.

Mab. Tho' scarcely audible, his favorite air.

Priest. Her eyes with an unearthly lustre beam—

    Glimpses of consciousness seem mingling there,

    Yet there is nothing that she surely knows.

Lady C. What is the hour?

Mab. The sun is in the west.

Lady C. Oh, let me see him sink behind the hills:
 Mabel, lead me: Kenneth!

Mab. Alas, sweet lady!
      [*She is assisted to the window.*

Lady C. He sets in glory—never scene so fair
 Blessed mortal eyes. 'Tis gone. Oh, I am sick!
 To me he never rises more. Mabel, my couch!
      [*She is laid upon her couch.*

Priest. The parting soul hath visions, it is said,
 Of glorious truth denied to healthy minds.

    [*Enter* LIDDESDALE.

Liddes. Loss upon loss accumulates. What next?
 That counterfeiting mute torments my thoughts—
 There is much more in him than I admired.
 How is my daughter?

Priest. Sinking fast away.

Liddes. Rather would I be told, O Priest, she's dead,
 Than in the fearful struggle see her die.
      [*He approaches the couch.*
 Pale, pale that face—its wondrous light is gone:
 While in this world there still is hope.

Priest. Amen!
 I've watched the live-long night, in fervent prayer
 She might revive to hear the gospel truths!

Liddes. She breathes more freely; see, her eyes unclose.
 Dost know me, child?

Lady C. Father !

Liddes. Oh, my daughter !

Lady C. Thy hands are bloody still: it is no dream!

Liddes. [*To Mabel.*] There, gently, gently; lay her
    softly down.

Lady C. I see them still arrayed in robes of white;
    A dear one, stateliest of the sainted throng,
    Is calling me.   Hark, hark, delightful strains!
    Prolong, prolong!   The vaulty space is filled
    With shadowy shapes, like vestals at the shrine—
    An angel in the midst supremely blest.
    O holy sight !   I mingle with thy train!

                                [*Dies.*

Priest. With that soft sigh her spirit passed away!

Liddes. Is there no hope on earth nor help in heaven!
    For him and for my promise did I strike,
    But like the blind, I overshot the mark
    And killed my innocent child!

Mab. Oh, woe is me !

Liddes. I did not think grief could subdue me thus.

Priest. Thou hast a friend in heaven—an angel there—
    Pleading thy pardon at the Eternal throne.

Liddes. Oh, I have heard men groan and women wail;
    Waded in blood, yet never felt a pang—
    But, in the death of this dear child, I feel
    Ten thousand furies tearing at my heart.
    She'll never smile on me again: never!
    And I am left to bustle through the world

In this calamity.   No time to weep.
Mabel, gently—she was a gentle child—
[*To the Priest.*] Treat her poor dust as doth become
   her rank,
And bear her to the grave with saddest pomp.
Call in my people: they may weep and wail,
For their dear mistress now is with the saints,
And I am left alone—alone, lamenting.

                         [*Curtain falls.*

6

ACT V.

Scene I.—*The Wardens' Tent. Martial Music. Enter* Lord Wm. Dacre, Sir John Charters, Lord Maxwell, Carnegie, *Heralds, Lords, Soldiers and Attendants.*

Sir John Ch. Altho' our royal master fain would spare
    The flow of native blood—tho' he would see
    The fields of spring to harvest grow apace,
    And all his people live in thrifty peace;
    He never will permit ambitious lords
    In arrogant pride to spurn allegiance due.
    Now we must teach this rash, misguided man
    The price of his presumption; he must feel,
    And all who league with him, just punishment;
    Which to inflict, with confidence we march.
    Thy gracious sovereign, whom may heaven preserve,
    Is rich in such a leader: thanks we owe
    For sagest counsel.
Lord D. What is the rebel force?   [strong;
Sir John Ch. But yesterday 'twas twenty thousand
    To-day, not half: he has affronted Hume,
    And thence his loss.
Lord D. Hume and his friends secure.

Send forth a Herald, through the land proclaim,
To those who join our standard in three days,
A pardon free for all offences past ;
And threaten those with death and confiscation,
Who aid the rebel or refuse submission.

Sir John Ch. I like thy counsel, let it be proclaimed.

                                [Exit a Herald.

Lord Max. I was the father of as brave a boy
As ever woman bore : he was my eldest born,
And loved—my lords, these tears attest how much,
More than my words.

Sir John Ch. We do lament his death,
And in the common cause we will avenge it.

Lord Max. His bleeding corse by this brave-hearted man
Was from his merciless murderer reclaimed ;
What to preserve him he essayed, ye know :
What he devised to wring the rebel's heart,
What of his plans disclosed, ye also know.
Now to reward his valor, honor, truth,
I crave a boon.

Sir John Ch. My lord, thy grief commands
More than thy frosted head.

Lord Max. Ennoble him!
Noble his deeds—make him the like in rank.

Sir John Ch. Kneel down, Carnegie, this old knight
commands.

        *[*CARNEGIE *kneels: a Herald holds the royal
              banner over him: the Warden lays a
              sword on his shoulder.*

Thus, in St. Andrew's name, I dub thee knight:
Sir John Carnegie of Eskhill arise—
Be loyal, bold and true.

[*A flourish.*

                                            Sir Herald, find
A proper crest to blazon on his shield.

Lord Max. Be generous, sir.

Herald. New knight, I name thy crest,
A bloody dagger clenched in rampant hand,
"*Ulciscar*" be the motto,

Lord Max. Fitly chosen.   [schooled,

Sir J. Carn. Permit me, noble lords, rude and un-
(Whose honors far outweigh his best desert,)
To ask translation of that foreign word
The learned Herald chooses for my crest.

Herald. In English, sir, it means, *I will revenge.*

Sir J. Carn. Bright thought, great thought—O glo-
rious word, revenge!
My lord, grant from thy vassals I may pick
A few brave, stalwart men to follow me,
For I have nothing—naked, as I stand.

Lord Max. 'Tis granted, sir; go forth, unfurl thy
pennon :
My best and bravest I entrust to thee.
I'm old; fond, frail and old. Would I were young!
My second son sojourns in vine-clad France;
Would he were home—be thou his proxy, sir.

Sir John Ch. A triple cause impels thee to the fight.

Lord Max. Avenge our king's, my son's, thy sister's
  wrongs.

Sir J. Carn. Three or four score, of sinew like the
  oak's,
  May join me from our hills; and I shall win
  A title to my crest, or die attempting.

Lord Max. And I will furnish thee befitting arms
  To win a soldier's name.

Lord D. Methinks this rebel
  (To whose undaunted heart some praise is due),
  Will deem we shrink afraid, unless forthwith
  We force submission at his castle gate.

Sir John Ch. A wise suggestion.

Lord D. And, to teach the land
  That treason is a crime not less 'gainst heaven
  Than heaven's anointed king, let no delay,
  No indecisive field leave room to doubt
  Where the advantage lies—crush him at once.

Sir John Ch. The while our soldiers seek some needful
  rest—
  A day at most—let our new knight, Sir John,
  Muster the men he wills. At dawn to-morrow,
  Our bugles sound advance : till then, to tents.
  　　　　　　　　　　　　[Martial music: exeunt.

SCENE II.—*A Court in* LIDDEL CASTLE.

[*Enter* LIDDESDALE.

Liddes. Now cursed be crones and damned all babbling
    rhymes,
      I dare in fate's despite.   Ah, childless now!
      Why am I spared with breath to speak that word!
      And Hume deserts me: let the villain rot!
      Cold as the sod, and I am all alone!
               [*Enter* LOCHWOOD.

Loch. The royal host advancing, at Langholm
      Halted for further aid.

Liddes. Let them advance—
      We are a handful, but in heart a host.
      What is their force?

Loch. One just arrived, reports,
      Of bows and lances, pikes and barbed horse,
      They are ten thousand strong.

Liddes. Out, out and face them—
      The better shall we seem with means supplied:
      Foemen confronted well are half subdued.
      They double ours.

Loch. Thy castle's strength atones,
      Should fortune force us to seek shelter here.

Liddes. Better to hear the lark—you know the rest.
      Why then consult the safety of our walls,
      Till there is none without: or why permit

These royal slaves to ravage our demains
When we may feast luxuriously on theirs?
No more delay; with speed bring up thy troop:
Command that Armstrong, Elliot, Crawford,
　　Graham,
March with their power and join us at the Forest.
With swift dispatch away.　　[*Exit* LOCKWOOD.
　　　　　　　　　Tho' they advance
Strong as the waves or numerous as the leaves,
I'll meet them like the tempest.　Treacherous Hume,
Thy blood shall pay for this calamity—　　[thee
Cold by thy mother's side! I could have spared
Sooner or later—any time but this!
　　　　　[*Enter* KENNETH.
What speaks thy speed?

Ken. Lord Hume has joined the king.

Liddes. The king of Darkness.

Ken. The king of Scotland.　　　　　[*Exit.*

Liddes. False, leperous chief!　May earthquakes swal-
　　low him—
Brand him on earth as one to be abhorred—
Let him not taste the springs our cattle drink—
World be his wilderness—there let him howl!
　　　　　[*Enter a Messenger.*
Speak, sirrah, speak, my heart is all a-fire;
Fleet as the lightning speak, or as my rage.

Mess. The Wardens have issued a proclamation com-
　　manding all people to join the royal standard—

offering free pardon for offences past; and threatening those who either aid your Grace or hold
neutral with confiscation and death.   [*Exit.*

Liddes. By my soul's hope I am exceeding glad:
  We shall distinguish now our honest friends:
  'Twas this that turned the adder-hearted Hume;
  Live, wretched craven, live to fear thyself.

  [*Enter* LOCHWOOD.

Loch. Armstrong, they say, has joined the royal banner.

Liddes. Level Gilknockie with the ground! Let Ker
  Take heed that not one stone remains erect
  To tax its fellows with their master's treason.

Loch. What Ker, my lord! he is a traitor too.

Liddes. Cessford with fire and sword I will destroy—
  Gilknockie too: women and men and babes
  Alike, shall swell the slaughter.   Blood, O blood!
  Spare none—slay all—let procreators die!

  [*Enter another Messenger.*

Mess. Armstrong and forty gentlemen of note
  The king at Carlenrigg has hanged.

Liddes. Ha, ha!
  Why this is news—rare, happy, excellent news!
  Fellow, I shall reward thee for thy pains.
  And what of Hume and Cessford? Are they hanged?
  Let justice have her own and—they are doomed.

Mess. I have no news of them.   [*Exit.*

Loch. I always thought
  Armstrong would never die a natural death.

Liddes. Like him may traitors perish—an example
 That I shall follow—to the letter follow—
 On all whom fortune places in my power.
 Come on, my lord, for we must summon up
 The few still faithful.   By our Saviour's blood,
 The world shall feel I have not lived in vain!
          [*Exeunt.*

SCENE III.—ESKHILL, *before the* CARNEGIE COTTAGE.
 Enter SIR JOHN CARNEGIE, *in armor,*
   with several followers.

Sir J. Carn. In armor and a knight !   'Tis realized!
 And that which seemed impossible, is true.
 My friends, in me behold a man up-raised
 By sudden fate to be a crested knight :
 Those we revere as of the ancient stock,
 Who won for Scotland her exalted name,
 Are sprung from sires unknown; and we may be
 The ancestors of nobles.   But to the point—
 I have permission to select true hearts
 That pant to share the glory of this war,
 Beneath the newest pennon.   Time there was—
 'Twas yesterday, and each preceding day
 I count of manhood, that ye yielded me
 Respect and kind regard: I thank ye, friends.
 Now, I have wrongs and injuries to avenge
 Would make the forests wail, the mountains groan.

All nature shriek aloud—wilt follow me,
Tho' I am, save in title, like yourselves?
Omnes. We'll follow you to death!
Sir J. Carn. Brave friends, my thanks—
    Thanks from my soul—'tis all I have to offer. ·
    Each with his comrade come: collect a troop—
    Three or four score with broadsword, jack, and targe,
    And meet me by the Wardens' tent.
Omnes. We will.
Sir J. Carn. In every bonnet plant a rowan-twig—
    A reason I shall give—now, friends, dispatch—
    And meet me in an hour.   No more: farewell.
                              [*Exeunt followers.*
    Wronger and slayer, flinty-hearted lord,
    I will make thee the wonder of the world,
    And earn my motto or deserve a grave.   [*Exit.*

SCENE IV.—*Before   the   Wardens'   Tent: Trumpets.*
    Enter SIR JOHN CHARTERS, LORD WM. DACRE, *with*
    other Lords and followers.

Sir John Ch. I like thy counsel: we await him here.
    He vainly thinks that we are unprepared;
    The loyal never sleep.   Thou wilt command
    Thy sovereign master's troops, while I lead mine:
    And bold Buccleugh shall bear the royal standard.
Lord D. Agreed.   As I rode out an hour ago
    To view the vantage of the neighboring ground,

I chose e'en this as the selectest place
To fight and win. My lord, this rough-drawn map—
Observe, I but suggest—will show my plan.
Here, on this hill I shall bestow my bows;
And in that wood—an ambush—plant my horse.
Now mark—by yonder road he must advance—
Meet him with lance and spear, and bid thy troops
Seem to retreat dismayed—and thus entrap
His chosen men within my archers' reach—
Be sure each cloth-yard shaft will tell its tale—
Our ambush then will cut off his retreat,
And he is ours.

Sir John Ch. It is with skill devised.

Lord D. There never was so sweet a place to fight.

Sir John Ch. But, what if he advance not?

Lord D. Then, my lord,
Entice him onward as at Flodden field—
Pray, pardon me my lord—dispel all doubt,
He is already roused to desperation,
And will advance.

Sir John Ch. Here comes our newest knight,
And, by my faith, he is attended well.

> [*Enter* Sir John Carnegie *and followers,
> armed, and bearing his pennon. Each
> with a rowan-twig in his bonnet.*

Sir J. Carn. Here come we, lords, to win a soldier's
name.

Sir John Ch. Welcome to tent: these iron-nerved,
    stalwart men
    Will win thee glory—by my troth, they will.
Sir J. C. Give us our place—we bow to thy command.
Lord D. Might not these troopers draw the rebel on ?
    My lord, they seem of mettle. •
Sir J. Carn. Seem! they are.
Sir John Ch. We learn by scouts the traitor is advancing;
    Mark yonder pass, 'tis distant scarce two miles,
    Through that we would entrap him—thither march,
    Receive his onset and before him yield,
    As if ye ran in fear.
Sir J. Carn. Pardon, my lord!
    The rowan-branch is sworn to die—not yield.
    Beneath the rowan was young Maxwell slain,
    Beside the rowan was my sister drowned;
    Now by my bursting soul, each fellow here,
    Swore as he placed that emblem in his cap,
    To avenge the murders near the rowan-tree,
    Or die in the attempt.
Lord D. Calm thee, Sir John—
    We would not counsel any friend to flee
    Unless 'twas for a stratagem of war.
Sir John Ch. It is the order for the general weal,
    As in our plan arranged.
Sir J. Carn. Well: we shall yield.
Lord D. Be calm, not rash: retreat as if compelled.

Sir J. Carn. Beneath each twig there beats a dauntless
    heart—
    And now—altho' our first essay in arms—
    We shall obey our noble chief's command.
    But when thy bugle sounds?
Sir John Ch. Advance and fight.
Sir J. Carn. Each foe shall be a fragile blade of corn,
    We'll hew him down like reapers. Grant me, heaven,
    That I may face the foul, corrupted chief,
    And then—God save the just!
Sir John Ch. Behold yon signal.
    The rebel is advancing. Sir, thy place—
    On with thy troop.
Lord D. Disgrace is not in flight,
    But in its cause. The bravest may retreat.
                              [Exeunt.

SCENE V.—*The Battle-field: Alarums.* Sir John
    Carnegie *and followers retreat across the stage,*
    pursued by the men of Liddesdale. *Enter* Liddes-
    dale, Lochwood, *and other Lords.*

Liddes. Pursue, pursue, fleet as the wind pursue:
    No prisoners take, but wolf-like hunt for blood.
                         [Exeunt followers.
    Yon beauteous sun shines on a glorious day—
    I feel new life; the field is surely won.
Loch. I like not such a bloodless flight.

Liddes. Cowards !
  All cowards to the core.
Loch. That is not proved :
  Such stout-framed men to run ere blood is spilt,
  Ere scarce a spear is crossed or broadsword hacked,
  Is strange and odd.   I think it a device.
Liddes. This busy day is one to strike, not think.
Loch. They fought defensive, willing to retreat—
  Their faces showed no evidence of fear.
Liddes. If our true men are swift, not one escapes.
Loch. Why, any man may rush to the attack,
  Or follow those who flee; the boldest leader
  Is not alone intent to hurt his foe,
  But with a prudent eye surveys the field
  To make most havoc at the smallest cost.   [that:
  Look there—through yonder pass they run—mark
  Rugged and narrow: good place for ambush.
Liddes. Each inch of ground familiar to my step,
  Gives me advantage o'er their sagest schemes.
  Talk not of ambush—'tis not in their art,
  Nor in their cunning, on this land to snare me.
Loch. If I mistake, then level me with serfs.
  Danger is here ; call the pursuers back.
Liddes. Does Lochwood counsel me to spare a foe ?
Loch. Yon troop is by a stranger chieftain led,
  Whose blazoned shield displays an unknown crest;
  Whether he be of Scotland, England, France,
  Or what his birth or rank, we nothing know.

Liddes. Perhaps a traitor fights in this disguise—
Belike 'tis Ker, or deeper damned than he,
Abhorred Hume! Perhaps the king himself!
Loch. What 'vantage or renown would'st thou achieve
In conquering him? Seek out the royal banner,
And lion-like among thy peers contend.
He is not worth thy blow.
Liddes. Were he a—devil,
I'm eager for encounter hand to hand.
There is an angel or a demon here,
Spurring my soul 'gainst this mysterious knight:
I'm yearning for his blood. Tho' nature wept,
And universal man in one loud voice
Cried out, forbear! I should not stop my course.
Loch. Amuse them till the forty days expire.
Liddes. I will not wait—no, not for forty moments.
Now, as we are, advance: bring up thy power—
Or, if thou fear'st to fight, go beg thy life
Like Ker and Hume, or be like Armstrong hanged.
This day shall prove my greatest or my last.
[*Exeunt.*

SCENE VI.—*Another part of the field.*   *Alarums.*
Enter LIDDESDALE.

Liddes. Strike as I may, each well-concerted blow,
    By adverse chance is turned against myself
    As fate were leagued against me.   What, ambush!
    Like him at Gaza, though I crush myself
    I'll tear the temple down.
                    [*Enter* LOCHWOOD *and other Lords.*
Loch. Our best are slain.
Liddes. If from the grave my father's ghost had risen
    And told me this, I would have sworn it lied.
    Ambush?   What day is this?
Loch. Wednesday, my lord.
Liddes. My luckless day!   Well, well!   I had forgot—
    It is begun, and it must labor through—
    Yet, had I listened—that is past recall.
    Send a fresh troop of horse around the marsh,
    And charge them in the rear.   [*Exit* LOCHWOOD.
    O heavy blow!
    Struck at the threshold of her womanhood;
    My only one, all hope of lineage gone !
    Pick me ten score of tried and trusty men
    To force by yonder wood the Blackburn pass,
    And drive the English archers from the hill.
    If they maintain that stand, the day is lost.
                    [*Exit an officer.*
    A horrid thought!   If I should chance to fall,
    My corse might be insulted.—How goes the day?

Re-enter LOCHWOOD.

Loch. Our troopers bravely fight, but fast as hail
    The southron bowmen pour their arrows down
    And each one takes a life.

Liddes. Another troop!
    Send out another, and another—all!
    And force them from the hill. Drag from the castle
    Warders and watchers, yea, each living soul,
    Whose strength can wield a sword or bear a spear.
                     [*Exit an officer.*
    One noble rally and we conquer yet.

Loch. Worse fields than this by daring have been won.

Liddes. Come to our work—havoc and death, come on.
    One word, to speak the heart's tormenting thought:
    Swear, if I fall, at cost of all the world,
    To rescue or to ransom me—swear this!
    Alive, all mortal aid I should despise,
    But on this luckless day my thrice-tried mail
    May by an English arrow be transfixed—
    Swear, if I die, my body you will burn,
    And strew its ashes to the wind—swear this!
    Let not a foe invade my castle halls—
    Let not my trophies be a prey to him—
    Burn, burn them to the ground, burn all: swear this!

Loch. If I survive, I swear it shall be done.

Liddes. Content: my thanks! Thou art my truest friend:
    All is not lost, we yet may win the day.
                     [*Exeunt.*

7

SCENE VII.—*The Rowan Tree. Bugles sound advance.*
Enter SIR JOHN CARNEGIE *and followers.*

Sir J. Carn. These thrilling sounds! On, rowan-branch,
   rush on!
   No more of flight! This is a day of glory,
   And he who serves his country in its need,
   Shall share the honor when the field is won.
   Avenging power! who in the appointed time
   Strikest down the guilty, me thy agent make!
   Temper my steel—bring him within its reach—
   And, as I then engage, if worthy thee,
   Give to my thirsting soul a sea of blood,
   For I could gorge it all! Now, like ourselves.
                     [*Exeunt.*
    [*A pause: Alarums. Enter* LIDDESDALE.
Liddes. If e'er I put one particle of faith
   In superstitious tales, I might believe
   The legend tells the downfall of my house,
   And this the day, by heaven ordained, to prove it.

      " When humble foes
        And high oppose—
        Listen "———

Thus runs the ancient rhyme—it seems like truth.
By friends deserted and by foes hemmed round—

High foes, a legion—where the humble ones?
I meet them not—the legend is a lie.

               [*Re-enter* SIR JOHN CARNEGIE.

Sir J. Carn. From first to last for thee alone I've sought.
And down struck scores, all profitless till now.

Liddes. What stranger knight art thou, who wildly comes
With more than mortal wrongs uproused.

Sir J. Carn. By my soul's wrath, a foe; a deadly foe,
Sworn while I live to live thy foe alone.

Liddes. Up with thy visor, sir; vain this disguise;
For dead or living I shall see thy face.
When first I saw thy pennon in the field,
Flying in terror with thy craven troop,
Thy presence blasted like an evil star:
Declare thy rank: I feel upon thy death
Depends the glory of this day.   Be brief—
I'll cleave thee down, and then for better blows.

Sir J. Carn. Unsuperstitious as thou think'st thou art,
Thou wilt with terror freeze to see my face.

Liddes. Wert thou a fiend in double mail disguised,
I would not shun thee: if thou art a knight——

Sir J. Carn. I am a knight—ennobled since the dawn.

Liddes. A new-made knight!   From what condition
    sprung?
With wherefore that blazon? speak!

Sir J. Carn. A Providence!
The hand of heaven is raised.   Behold the truth!

               [*Uncloses his visor.*

Liddes. My counterfeiting mute!

Sir J. Carn. Yes, yesterday:

    To-day, Sir John Carnegie of Eskhill,

    Thy equal and thy foe!

Liddes. Thou, lowborn cur!

    Hence from my sight—thou art not worth a blow.

    I seek the noble, not false slaves like thee.

Sir J. Carn. "*When humble foes*"—

Liddes. Hence, corbel-face! begone!

Sir J. Carn. Not while thou art alive!   O just revenge!

    Salacious wretch! here, by thy lust deflowered,

    A gentle maiden leaped into the stream;

    Here, by thy treacherous hand young Maxwell fell;

    And I am here, the instrument of heaven,

    Armed and ennobled, to avenge thy crimes.

Liddes. Presumest thou to threaten or rebuke?

    I am the Border Chief—my word, a law—

    My sword, a fate.   Villain, I spared thee once,

    And I should blush to soil this precious brand

    With dastard blood like thine.   Go find thy peer;

    I seek a noble or a royal foe.   [*grave,*

Sir J. Carn. A sister's ghost shrieks from the sheeted

    A desolate father for huge vengeance prays:

    I neither shriek nor pray—I come to do!

Liddes. Thou! perjured and accursed; stop not my

    course.   [*Going.*

Sir J. C. Turn not thy back, or die the coward's death;

And I will drag thy carcass by the heels,
The peasants wonder and the chieftains scorn;
And when their eyes are sated with the sight,
Will cast it, naked, to devouring wolves.   [left.
Liddes. Hold, insolent wretch! there's no redemption
Despite the legend, and though fame rebuke,
I will chastise thy overbearing pride,
And crush thee, like a reptile, 'neath my feet.
Thy blood is honored when it stains my sword.
Sir J. Carn. God, me defend.
                    [*They fight :* LIDDESDALE *falls.*
Liddes. 'Tis true: the legend's true.
This more ennobles thee than monarch's breath,
And I have fallen by an humble serf,
The last of all my race: my fame survives!
                    [*Trumpets sound a victory.*
What sounds are these! Lochwood, thy oath, thy
    oath.
Rescue or ransom. My child! Burn, burn, burn!
                              [*Dies.*
    [*Enter* SIR JOHN CHARTERS, LORD WM. DACRE,
        Lords, Soldiers, etc.
Sir John Ch. The field is ours, deep dyed in rebel blood,
And this the reddest spot. New knight, thy hand:
We shall report thy valor to the king,
And deeds of greatness. In his generous heart
Thou art ennobled through succeeding time.
                    [*Curtain falls.*

www.ingramcontent.com/pod-product-compliance
Lightning Source LLC
Chambersburg PA
CBHW030550270326
41927CB00008B/1588